THE FUNDAMENTALS OF

FENG SHUI

THE FUNDAMENTALS OF
FENG SHUI

LILLIAN TOO

Shaftesbury, Dorset • Boston, Massachusetts • Melbourne, Victoria

Compilation © Element Books Limited 1999

Text © Lillian Too 1999

This compliation first published in Great Britain in 1999 by
ELEMENT BOOKS LIMITED
Shaftesbury, Dorset SP7 8BP

Published in the USA in 1999 by
ELEMENT BOOKS INC
160 North Washington Street, Boston MA 02114

Published in Australia in 1999 by
ELEMENT BOOKS LIMITED
and distributed by Penguin Australia Ltd
487 Maroondah Highway, Ringwood, Victoria 3134

Designed and created with
THE BRIDGEWATER BOOK COMPANY LIMITED

ELEMENT BOOKS LIMITED
Editorial Director Sue Hook
Managing Editor Miranda Spicer
Group Production Director Clare Armstrong
Production Manager Stephanie Raggett

THE BRIDGEWATER BOOK COMPANY LIMITED
Art Director Terry Jeavons
Designer James Lawrence
Managing Editor Anne Townley
Project Editor Andrew Kirk
Editor Linda Doeser
Picture Research Julia Hanson
Studio Photography Guy Ryecart
Illustrations Isabel Rayner, Andrew Kulman, Mark Jamieson,
Michaela Blunden, Paul Collicutt, Olivia Rayner, Jackie Harland

Printed and bound in Italy

British Library Cataloguing in Publication data available

Library of Congress Cataloging in Publication data available

ISBN 1 86204 768 5

The publishers wish to thank the following for the use of pictures:
Bridgeman Art Library, pp 23, 199, 207, 212; Elizabeth Whiting Associates, pp 18, 20, 78, 81, 120,
133, 179, 180, 196, 230, 231; Julia Hanson, pp 17, 59, 157, 175, 190; Image Bank, pp 13, 39, 54,
56, 80/1, 159, 229, 233, 238; Rex, pp 110, 198; Wolfgang Kaehler/Corbis, p. 75; Zefa, pp 13, 15,
19, 23, 47, 57, 59, 67, 97, 98, 99, 102, 119, 123, 128, 134, 156, 157, 158, 163, 164, 165, 184, 200,
221, 223

Special thanks go to:
Bright Ideas, Lewes, East Sussex
for help with properties

Lillian Too's website address is:
www.lillian-too.com

CONTENTS

HOW TO USE THIS BOOK

This book is designed to help you understand the principles of the ancient art of feng shui, the culture it came from, and the ways in which you can apply the principles to your life.

The first part of the book covers the fundamentals of feng shui: what it means, how and why it works, and what it can do for you. This explains the major principles, such as the Pa Kua symbol, the eight trigrams, and the five elements. The theory is then put into practice in the subsequent sections, which show you how to interpret and use feng shui in the many arenas of your own life: wealth, love, fame, health, children, education, networking, and careers.

Charts enable you to work out your personal feng shui profile

Introductory spreads (below) clarify the fundamentals of the fascinating, 4,000-year-old art of feng shui.

Beautiful photographs illustrate the essence of the philosophy

INDIVIDUAL WE ORIENTATIO

THE COMPASS FORMULA

方位

Also known as the Pa Kua Lo Shu formula (Kua formula for short), this method of investigating personal prosperity orientations was given to the author's feng shui Master by old Taiwan feng shui Grand Master who was a legend in his time. As the personal consultant of many of Taiwan's richest men of the time, Master Chan Chuan Huay was an expert on wealth feng shui and was particularly well schooled in the science of water feng shui. He was also in possession of this Kua formula and used it with spectacular success for his clients, many of whom founded huge business conglomerates that are managed today by their heirs and descendants. It is no coincidence that the small island of Taiwan is so rich. Feng shui has always been widely practiced there.

riches. A f symbol, bu frog is t symbolize quite spe frogs are and so ar

THE THREE-LEGGED FROG

The three-legged frog with a coin in its mouth and surrounded by yet more coins signifies an abundance of

~84~

THE CHINESE VIEW OF THE LIVING EARTH

THE WINDS AND THE WATERS

風水

Feng shui means "wind and water." In the literal sense it refers to the topography of the earth: its mountains, valleys, and waterways, whose shapes and levels, are created by the continuous interaction of these two powerful forces of nature.

To people of Chinese origin all over the world, feng shui connotes a mystical practice that blends ancient wisdom with cultural superstitions. This broad body of traditional knowledge lays down guidelines for differentiating between auspicious and inauspicious land sites. It also provides instructions on how to orient homes and design room layouts to enhance the quality of life dramatically.

In the family home, well-oriented feng shui features work to create harmonious relationships between husband and wife and between children and parents, foster

good health, and attract abundance and prosperity. They bring good fortune to the breadwinner, build good reputations, and strengthen descendants' luck – children who will bring honor and happiness to the family in the future.

In business premises, good feng shui creates opportunities for growth, elevates prestige in the community, attracts customers, raises profits, and expands turnover. Employees stay loyal and a pervasive aura of goodwill ensures smooth working relationships.

Good feng shui results when the winds and the waters surrounding your home and work space are harmonious and well balanced. Bad feng shui, on the other hand, brings illness, disasters, accidents, burglaries, and financial loss. It results in lost opportunities, fading careers, squandered wealth, and collapsed reputations. Above all, bad feng shui causes grave unhappiness, and it can sometimes even provoke tragic consequences for the reputation and well-being of the family unit

~10~

as a whole.

WHAT IS FENG SHUI?

Feng shui advocates living in harmony with the earth's environment and energy lines so that there is balance with the forces of nature.

Feng shui contends that the environment is crowded with powerful, but invisible energy lines.

Feng shui says that some of these energy lines are auspicious, bringing great good fortune, while some are pernicious and hostile, bringing death and the destruction of happiness.

Feng shui offers ways of arranging the home so that these energy lines become

Positive energy would have difficulty accumulating in this barren, windswept landscape.

Good feng shui practice encourages good luck to flow through your home and touch all who live there, just as this meandering river flowing through the landscape nourishes the surrounding farmland.

harmonious and bring prosperity and harmony, rather than loss and discord.

Feng shui instructs us in the clever harnessing of auspicious energy lines – generally referred to as sheng chi, the dragon's cosmic breath – making sure they meander gently through the home and accumulate and settle, thereby bringing good fortune

Feng shui teaches us to avoid, deflect, and dissolve inauspicious energy lines – also known as shar chi – which represent the killing breath caused by secret poison arrows in the surroundings.

Feng shui strenuously warns against sleeping, working, sitting, eating, and

~11~

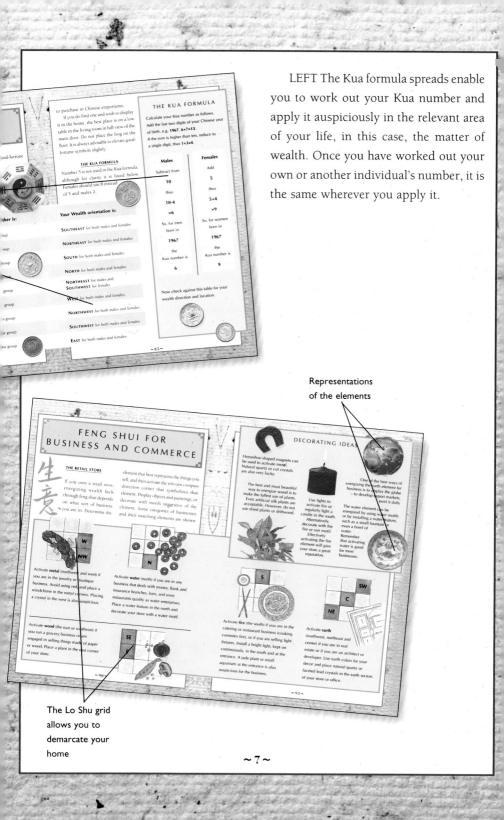

LEFT The Kua formula spreads enable you to work out your Kua number and apply it auspiciously in the relevant area of your life, in this case, the matter of wealth. Once you have worked out your own or another individual's number, it is the same wherever you apply it.

THE KUA FORMULA

to purchase in Chinese emporiums.

If you do find one and wish to display it in the home, the best place is on a low table in the living room in full view of the main door. Do not place the frog on the floor. It is always advisable to elevate good-fortune symbols slightly.

THE KUA FORMULA

Number 5 is not used in the Kua formula, although for clarity it is listed below. Females should use 8 instead of 5 and males 2.

Your Wealth orientation is:

SOUTHEAST for both males and females

NORTHEAST for both males and females

SOUTH for both males and females

NORTH for both males and females

NORTHEAST for males and SOUTHWEST for females

WEST for both males and females

NORTHWEST for both males and females

SOUTHWEST for both males and females

EAST for both males and females

Calculate your Kua number as follows. Add the last two digits of your Chinese year of birth, e.g. 1967. 6+7=13. If the sum is higher than ten, reduce to a single digit, thus 1+3=4.

Males	Females
Subtract from	Add
10	5
thus	thus
10-4	5+4
=6	=9
So, for men born in	So, for women born in
1967	1967
the Kua number is	the Kua number is
6	9

Now check against this table for your wealth direction and location.

~ 85 ~

FENG SHUI FOR BUSINESS AND COMMERCE

生意

THE RETAIL STORE

If you own a retail store, energizing wealth luck through feng shui depends on what sort of business you are in. Determine the element that best represents the things you sell, and then activate the relevant compass direction corner that symbolizes that element. Display objects and paintings, or decorate with motifs suggestive of the element. Some categories of businesses and their matching elements are shown

Activate **metal** (northwest and west) if you are in the jewelry or boutique business. Avoid using red and place a windchime in the metal corners. Placing a crystal in the west is also auspicious.

Activate **water** (north) if you are in any business that deals with money. Bank and insurance branches, bars, and even restaurants qualify as water enterprises. Place a water feature in the north and decorate your store with a water motif.

Activate **wood** (the east or southeast) if you run a grocery business or are engaged in selling things made of paper or wood. Place a plant in the east corner of your store.

Activate **fire** (the south) if you are in the catering or restaurant business (cooking connotes fire), or if you are selling light fixtures. Install a bright light, kept on continuously, in the south and at the entrance. A jade plant or small aquarium at the entrance is also auspicious for the business.

Activate **earth** (southwest, northeast and center) if you are in real estate or if you are an architect or developer. Use earth colors for your decor and place natural quartz or faceted lead crystals in the earth sectors of your store or office.

~ 90 ~

DECORATING IDEAS

Horseshoe-shaped magnets can be used to activate metal. Natural quartz or cut crystals are also very lucky.

The best and most beautiful way to energize wood is to make the fullest use of plants. Even artificial silk plants are acceptable. However, do not use dried plants or driftwood.

Use lights to activate fire or regularly light a candle in the south. Alternatively, decorate with the fire or sun motif. Effectively activating the fire element will give your store a great reputation.

One of the best ways of energizing the earth element for business is to display the globe — to develop export markets, and twirl it daily.

The water element can be energized by using water motifs, or by installing a water feature, such as a small fountain or even a bowl of water. Remember that activating water is good for most businesses.

~ 91 ~

Representations of the elements

The Lo Shu grid allows you to demarcate your home

~ 7 ~

Feng Shui
Fundamentals

The
Fundamentals

THE CHINESE VIEW
OF THE LIVING EARTH

THE WINDS AND THE WATERS

Feng shui means "wind and water." In the literal sense it refers to the topography of the earth: its mountains, valleys, and waterways, whose shapes and sizes, orientation, and levels, are created by the continuous interaction of these two powerful forces of nature.

To people of Chinese origin all over the world, feng shui connotes a mystical practice that blends ancient wisdom with cultural superstitions. This broad body of traditional knowledge lays down guidelines for differentiating between auspicious and inauspicious land sites. It also provides instructions on how to orient homes and design room layouts to enhance the quality of life dramatically.

In the family home, well-oriented feng shui features work to create harmonious relationships between husband and wife and between children and parents, foster good health, and attract abundance and prosperity. They bring good fortune to the breadwinner, build good reputations, and strengthen descendants' luck – children who will bring honor and happiness to the family in the future.

In business premises, good feng shui creates opportunities for growth, elevates prestige in the community, attracts customers, raises profits, and expands turnover. Employees stay loyal and a pervasive aura of goodwill ensures smooth working relationships.

Good feng shui results when the winds and the waters surrounding your home and work space are harmonious and well balanced. Bad feng shui, on the other hand, brings illness, disasters, accidents, burglaries, and financial loss. It results in lost opportunities, fading careers, squandered wealth, and collapsed reputations. Above all, bad feng shui causes grave unhappiness, and it can sometimes even provoke tragic consequences for the reputation and well-being of the family unit as a whole.

WHAT IS FENG SHUI?

Feng shui advocates living in harmony with the earth's environment and energy lines so that there is balance with the forces of nature.

Feng shui contends that the environment is crowded with powerful, but invisible, energy lines.

Feng shui says that some of these energy lines are auspicious, bringing great good fortune, while some are pernicious and hostile, bringing death and the destruction of happiness.

Feng shui offers ways of arranging the home so that these energy lines become harmonious and bring prosperity and harmony, rather than loss and discord.

Good feng shui practice encourages good luck to flow through your home and touch all who live there, just as this meandering river flowing through the landscape nourishes the surrounding farmland.

Positive energy would have difficulty accumulating in this barren, windswept landscape.

Feng shui instructs us in the clever harnessing of auspicious energy lines – generally referred to as sheng chi, the dragon's cosmic breath – making sure they meander gently through the home and accumulate and settle, thereby bringing good fortune.

Feng shui teaches us to avoid, deflect, and dissolve inauspicious energy lines – also known as shar chi – which represent the killing breath caused by secret poison arrows in the surroundings.

Feng shui strenuously warns against sleeping, working, sitting, eating, and generally living in places that are hit by these pernicious hostile energy lines.

THE LANDSCAPES OF THE WORLD

Feng shui is an exciting component of ancient Chinese wisdom – a science that goes back at least 4,000 years to the days of the emperors and mythical legends. That it has so brilliantly survived the centuries bears testimony to its potency. In recent years there has been an extensive revival of interest in its practice, particularly in the West, where the study of feng shui began as a New Age phenomenon, but has now attracted mainstream attention.

The current popularity of feng shui stems from the widespread appeal of its simple logic. While its many theories and guidelines are based on the Chinese view of the universe, the fundamentals are easily understood and widely applicable. Its laws and tenets relate to simple basic concepts that advocate living harmoniously with the environment, creating balance in the living space, and blending in with the natural landscapes of the world: the contours of the land, the terrain of the earth, the rivers, and waterways of the world, sunlight and moonlight, vegetation, orientations, and directions – in short, the winds and waters of the living earth that surrounds us.

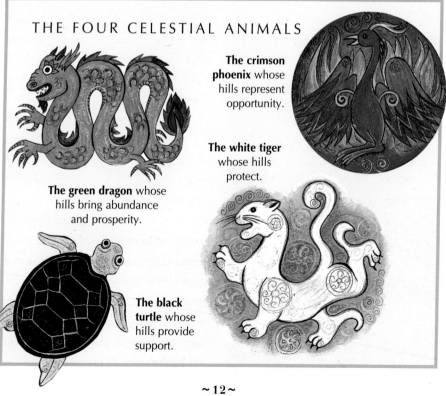

THE FOUR CELESTIAL ANIMALS

The crimson phoenix whose hills represent opportunity.

The white tiger whose hills protect.

The green dragon whose hills bring abundance and prosperity.

The black turtle whose hills provide support.

CLASSICAL FENG SHUI

A fundamental tenet of feng shui advises you to live with your back to a mountain. So if your home is backed by something solid and firm, such as a hill or a building that simulates the hill, you will have support all your life. Thus the first part of classical feng shui is to have the mountain behind.

There should be open space in front of your home, so that your vision is not hampered and your horizon is visible. If there is also a view of water, it brings auspicious energy into your living area. Moreover, if the river is slow moving and meandering, the good energy has a chance to settle and accumulate before entering your home, thereby allowing you to partake of its essence. Needless to say, the cleaner, fresher, and more sparkling the

This house, safely nestled among protective undulating green hills, enjoys the support of mountains in the background and the auspicious energy of nearby water.

water, the greater the good fortune that it will bring. Thus, the second half of classical feng shui says have water in front of your home.

In the lyrical language of the ancients, this classical feng shui configuration describes the mountain behind as the black turtle hills and the river in front, with its footstool of a hillock, as the phoenix hills. On the left, feng shui introduces the important green dragon, a range of hills that is gentle and undulating, while on the right are the lower white tiger hills. The symbolism of these four celestial animals describes classical feng shui landscape configuration. If your home is comfortably nestled within the bosom of these four animals, you will be supported by the black turtle, made prosperous by the green dragon, protected by the white tiger, and brought wonderful opportunities by the crimson phoenix.

The optimum feng shui configuration looking from the house:
black turtle hills behind for support; the crimson phoenix hill in front for good luck; the green dragon hills, on the left for prosperity; and smaller hills, the white tiger, on the right for protection.

THE FUNDAMENTALS
OF FENG SHUI

THE HARMONY
OF YIN AND YANG ENERGIES

風水

At its most basic, feng shui is a question of balance, but this balance is related to the complementarity of opposites, expressed in terms of the yin and the yang. According to the Chinese, all things in the universe are either the female yin or the male yang, the dark yin or the bright yang.

Yin and yang together make up the wholeness of the universe, which includes heaven and earth. Yin and yang breathe meaning into each other, for without one, the other cannot exist. Thus, without the yin of darkness, there cannot be the light of yang, without the cold temperature of yin, there cannot possibly be the warmth of yang – and vice versa.

When there is balance between the yin and yang, the wholeness of the universe is represented. There is good balance and prosperity, health, well-being, and happiness. Feng shui practice always includes a yin-yang analysis of room space, land configurations, sunlight and shade, dampness and dryness, bright and pale colors, and solids and fluids. Rooms that are too yin are not auspicious; there are insufficient life energies to bring prosperity. Rooms that are too yang are said to be damaging because there is too much energy, causing accidents and huge losses. Only rooms – and homes – with balanced yin and yang can be auspicious and will be made even more auspicious if there is a good balance of yin and yang outside.

The ancient Chinese symbol of yin and yang represents the delicate interplay of complementary opposites that underpins the structure of the whole universe.

Graveyards, and other places associated with death, are full of strong yin energy that is passed on to nearby houses and buildings.

HOMES THAT ARE TOO YIN

Houses and buildings built too near graveyards, hospitals, prisons, slaughter-houses, and police stations are too yin because such places are associated with the yin energies of death. Even places of worship, such as temples, churches, and mosques, are said to give out extreme yin energies because of the rituals associated with mourning held there. The same diagnosis is often pronounced on buildings that are located on land that previously housed these places making it advisable to research the history of your home.

REMEDIES

It is better to avoid living in such yin places, but if you really cannot help it, then there are some remedies.

- Orient your main door so that it faces away from the yin structure or building.
- Do not have windows that open toward these yin structures.
- Paint your door bright red to signify strong, powerful yang energy.
- Make sure your porch is always well lit. Keep the light on all the time.
- Bring in the yang sunlight by cutting back shady trees.
- Plant trees with luscious vegetation and grow flowers in the garden.
- Put garden lights all round the house.
- Paint your fence a bright, happy color.
- Make sure you have a red roof.
- Introduce yang objects, such as boulders, pebbles, and stones, into the garden.

Large, unobstructed windows help to dissipate the excess yin energy that can accumulate in small, cramped rooms.

ROOMS THAT ARE TOO YIN

Rooms that never see sunlight, are damp, decorated in only shades of gray and blue, narrow and cramped, always closed and silent, or which have been occupied for a long time by someone who has been chronically sick, have too much yin energy. They cause sickness and bad luck to befall the residents. People who stay in rooms that have an excess of yin energy suffer more than their fair share of misfortunes and seem to be shrouded by a cloak of ill luck.

CREATING YANG ENERGY

Try to create some yang energy by doing the following.

- Repaint the walls with a bright yang color – pinks, yellows, even red.
- Bring in the light. White walls are very yang because they are bright.
- Throw away draping curtains and bring the sunlight into the room.
- Use happy colors for your curtains.
- Use bright colors for duvets, bed sheets and other soft furnishings.
- Keep the windows open.
- If trees are blocking the light from outside, cut them back.
- Install plenty of lights and keep at least one turned on continuously.
- Keep the radio or television turned on. Sound, life, and laughter bring in yang energy.
- Have vases of freshly cut flowers.
- Introduce movement with mobiles and wind chimes. They symbolize life energy.

Electrical transmission pylons and overhead wires can overwhelm homes with too much yang energy.

HOMES THAT ARE TOO YANG

Buildings that are constantly exposed to bright sunlight or heat of any kind are said to have an excess of yang energy, to the extent that it brings accidents, disasters, and grave misfortune. If you are living too near an electrical transmitter, or you are within view of large factory or refinery chimneys that belch noxious smoke throughout the day, there is too much yang energy.

It is advisable to move from such a place, but if you have no choice, then it is necessary – indeed vital – that you combat the excess yang energy by introducing yin structures or surround yourself with the colors and characteristics of yin. Water is one of the best cures for too much yang energy; creating a small pond of water in the garden will effectively counter the yang energy.

REMEDIES

Remedies for too much yang energy.

- Paint your door in any shade of blue, as this is a yin color.
- Select muted, cool colors for your interior decor.
- Avoid too much noise in the house.
- Avoid too much light in the house, and never have a red light turned on.
- Introduce water features, such as miniature fountains.
- Hang paintings of lakes and rivers in your home.
- Maintain a good lawn in your garden.
- Paint railings and gates black, as this, too, is a yin color.

ROOMS THAT ARE TOO YANG

If you play loud music all day long and your room is fitted with bright red furnishings and the walls are painted red or bright yellow, the energies are too yang. There is too much noise and too much energy, so you would be well advised to introduce some yin features to counter this imbalance. Observe some periods of silence during the day. Change your drapes to a darker yin color or even install a blue light.

This black and white color scheme creates a harmony of opposites.

Similarly, if your room receives direct hot afternoon sun, the room is too yang. Counter this by hanging some heavier drapes that cut out the glare of the sun. Or hang a faceted crystal that transforms the hostile sunlight into the bright colors of the rainbow, bringing in friendly yang energy rather than killing yang energy. Observe that creating a balance of yin and yang in your home is an extremely subtle exercise.

Essentially, a room should have elements of yin and yang but never too much of one or the other. Have music and life in the room, but not all the time. Have peace and quiet in the room, but not to the extent it becomes lifeless. Have a cool decor of blues and grays, but also incorporate a splash of yang color which may be represented by a vase of red roses or a painting of a sunrise.

Black and white color schemes are symbolic of yin and yang harmony, but there should also be sounds and life. A completely black and white decor that is always silent is regarded as much too yin in the same way that if there is too much noise, it is regarded as too yang.

Remember that feng shui is a subtle blend of opposite energies that complement each other. What you should always strive for is the harmony of opposites. This is the fundamental guiding principle of yin and yang.

THE EIGHT-SIDED PA KUA SYMBOL

This is probably the most important symbol of feng shui. The eight sides represent many things in the practice of feng shui, and by itself, it is also believed to symbolize powerful protective energies. Chinese people around the world hang the Pa Kua, above their main doors just outside their homes to guard against any killing energy that may inadvertently be shooting at them. This is usually caused by hostile objects or structures that represent poison arrows (see pages 40–47).

In the vocabulary of feng shui, the Pa Kua used as a protective symbol is the Pa Kua of the Early Heaven Arrangement. This has the trigrams arranged around the eight sides in a different way from the Pa Kua of the Later Heaven Arrangement. (see illustrations). The Early Heaven Pa Kua is also used in the practice of yin feng shui – the feng shui of grave sites for one's ancestors. The Chinese believe that the luck of descendants is hugely affected by the feng shui of their ancestors' graves.

For yang feng shui – the feng shui of the dwellings of the living, which is what concerns most of us – the symbol of the Later Heaven Pa Kua is significant. Here the arrangement of the trigrams around the eight sides gives meaning to the eight major directions of the compass represented on the Pa Kua, with south always placed at the top. It allows for the correct interpretation and relationships of the other symbols of feng shui.

These other symbols are associated with numbers (one to nine), the five elements (water, fire, earth, wood, and metal), the members of the family (father, mother, sons, and daughters), the celestial animals (turtle, dragon, tiger, and phoenix), and the characteristics of each of the eight trigrams themselves.

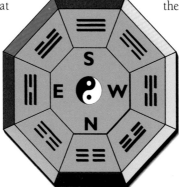

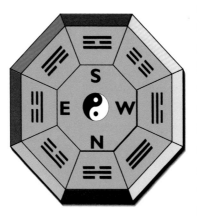

The Pa Kua of the Early Heaven
Arrangement (above)
and of the Later Heaven
Arrangement (below).

THE EIGHT TRIGRAMS AROUND THE PA KUA

Chien is probably the most powerful of the eight trigrams. This symbol of three solid unbroken lines represents heaven, the patriarch, the leader, and the father. In the Pa Kua it is placed northwest in the Later Heaven Arrangement. Consequently, the northwest is said to represent the patriarch or the person from whom all power emanates. For yang dwellings, houses of the living, the power of the household is said to come from the northwest and hence this is the location of the head of the household. This trigram is yang.

Kun is the archetype of the maternal or mother earth. This is the symbol of yielding, represented by three broken yin lines. It is thus completely yin. In the Pa Kua it is placed southwest and it signifies all things female – domesticity, docility, and maternal instincts. The matriarch of the family is best placed in the southwest for all her noblest qualities to flourish and for it to bring good fortune to the family.

Chen, two broken yin lines above a solid yang line, is the trigram placed east in the arrangement around the Pa Kua. It signifies the season of spring, the quality of growth, and embodies the spirit of the first male descendant. In the palaces of the Chinese emperors in Beijing's Forbidden City, the male heirs to the throne resided in the east of the palace complex. In any home this, too, is where the eldest son of the family should reside.

Sun, two solid yang lines above a broken yin line, is the trigram that embodies the spirit of the eldest daughter. Located in the southeast, it also signifies the wood element and the virtue of gentleness. The wind that brings prosperity is also located in the southeast.

Ken signifies stillness, the mountain. Represented by two broken yin lines lying just beneath the surface of the solid yang line, this trigram also denotes a place of preparation. Here, too, the place of the youngest son is symbolized. The location is northeast.

Kan also spells danger. Placed north, this trigram comprises a single solid yang line, surrounded by two broken yin lines, which signify the warmth of yang trapped by the cold of yin. Thus, Kan signifies winter and symbolizes water within which things are hidden. Kan represents the second son of the family.

Tui is the symbol of joyousness, represented by two solid yang lines about to break through the single yin line above. The season is fall, the direction is west and it represents the lake. The family member represented is the youngest daughter, who brings much joy and pleasure.

Li is placed in the south, opposite Kan. Here two solid yang lines trap the broken yin line, signifying the triumph of yang over yin. The element of this trigram is fire and the season is summer. Li signifies the brightness and beauty of summer. It is a trigram full of hope and it signifies the second daughter.

THE CONCEPT OF CHI

The abstract concept of chi penetrates all branches of Chinese traditional practice. Chi has no form, no shape, and is invisible, yet through it, all things on earth that affect people's well-being manifest themselves. Physical decay is the disintegration of chi and gradual death is the total absence of it.

Traditional Chinese practices, whether feng shui, acupuncture, or chi kung, all focus on protecting and nourishing chi, both externally and internally. Chi kung teaches that nourishing chi within through internal exercises effectively supplements health and longevity. Similarly the protection of chi inside the home will lead to harmony, prosperity, and longevity.

These ideas are based on the belief that all things in the universe, both alive and inanimate, possess chi. Every room, every house, every building – all natural and manmade spaces – are believed to contain energy that has its own unique form of chi. In external environments, the quality of chi is affected by the nature of the land – mountains, hills, and rivers – while inside the home, the quality of chi varies depending on its orientation, the items present in each room, as well as how they are arranged in relation to each other. Thus analyzing the landscape becomes important in assessing external feng shui and scrutinizing the orientation of the home and the arrangement of furniture becomes highly significant in interior feng shui.

The placement of entrances, exits, doors, and windows all affect the quality of the chi: whether it is vibrant, fresh, and alive with energy or stale and fatigued, hostile or damaging. Doors, especially main doors, become particularly crucial in the practice of feng shui.

The corners and center of any room have subtle variations in the type of chi present. This reflects the influence of the five elements, a theory of Chinese abstract thought. All things on earth are categorized into five elements, from compass directions and locations to different internal organs of the body, from seasons to mountain ranges. Thus, there will be fire chi, water chi, earth chi, metal chi, and wood chi. These types of chi affect different aspects of the human condition and their subtle activation represents one of the most interesting dimensions of feng shui practice.

MATCHING HUMAN CHI
TO ENVIRONMENTAL CHI

Once you know your personal family luck direction and you have demarcated the floor area of your house according to the Lo Shu square, there are several ways in which you can start to match your individual chi energies with that of your environment. You can activate your directions and attract auspicious sheng chi for the benefit of your whole family, especially if you are the main breadwinner.

Your Kua number, derived from the table on page 41, tells you your most auspicious direction for ensuring that you will not be lacking in children and descendants-luck. It also identifies the luckiest compass location for you to site your main door and your bedroom so as to make sure you capture smooth and harmonious sheng chi.

THE MASTER BEDROOM
AND THE SLEEPING DIRECTION

Perhaps the best way of acquiring happy family luck is to try to match all the most important doors according to the nien yen directions of the people in your family who use the rooms, especially the bedrooms. If you are the breadwinner, you will need to sleep with your head pointing in your nien yen direction. This means locating the master bedroom in the nien yen sector.

This gentle and beautiful sculpture which symbolizes parental love and mutual caring between parents and children would enhance the descendents luck of any home.

THE FIVE ELEMENTS

A core concept of feng shui practice is the theory of the five elements and their productive and destructive cycles. All Chinese astrological sciences, acupuncture, physical exercises such as chi kung, and medicine depend on an understanding of this theory for diagnosis and cures. In feng shui, understanding the nature and cycles of the elements vividly enhances the potency of its practice. This is because the Chinese view all things in the universe as belonging to one of the element groups. As each compass direction has its own ruling element, every corner of every home or room is also deemed to belong to one of these elements. The five elements are wood, fire, water, metal, and earth.

Feng shui practice takes account of element relationships by ensuring that the elements of objects, directions, and locations in any room do not destroy each other. Element relationships, based on their productive and destructive cycles, must, therefore, always be taken into account when any feng shui diagnosis or cure is being considered.

THE ELEMENTS

FIRE is red, considered a very auspicious yang color. Its season is summer and its direction is south. Symbols of this element are bright lights. Its number is nine. Fire animals are the snake and the horse.

WOOD is represented by all shades of green. Its season is spring. Big wood lies in the east, while small wood is in the southeast. Symbols of the wood element are plants, paper, furniture, and all things made of wood. In numerology, wood is represented by the numbers three and four. The Chinese horoscope lists the tiger and the rabbit as wood animals.

WATER is blue or black. Its season is winter and its direction is north. This is a yin element and its number is one. Objects that represent water include aquariums and fountains. Animals belonging to this element are the rat and the boar.

PRODUCTIVE AND DESTRUCTIVE CYCLES

PRODUCTIVE CYCLE
Each element creates the next in the cycle

WATER · WOOD · FIRE · EARTH · METAL

DESTRUCTIVE CYCLE
Each element destroys the next in the cycle

METAL · WOOD · EARTH · WATER · FIRE

In the productive cycle of the elements, fire produces earth, which creates metal, which makes water, which produces wood, which makes fire.

In the destructive cycle of elements, wood devours earth, which destroys water, which extinguishes fire, which consumes metal, which demolishes wood.

Try superimposing the destructive cycle of the elements above right on to the productive cycle above left. Start with wood at the top, move to earth below, up to water, across to fire, down to metal and back up to wood. You will find that you draw a five pointed star on to the productive cycle similar to the pentacle symbol of many ancient spiritual and religious practices.

EARTH is represented by all shades of brown. It is the element of the center and it represents every third month of every season. Its directions are southwest (big earth) and northeast (small earth). Its numbers are two, five, and eight and its horoscope animals are the ox, the dragon, the sheep, and the dog.

METAL is signified by the metallic colors, gold or silver, and also white. Its season is fall and its directions are west (small metal) and northwest (big metal). Objects of the element are wind chimes, bells, coins, and jewelry. Its numbers are six and seven. The metal animals of the Chinese horoscope are the rooster and the monkey.

THE LO SHU SQUARE
AND THE MAGIC OF NUMBERS

The Lo Shu square is another important symbol widely used in feng shui analysis, especially in the application of various compass feng shui formulas.

This nine-sector grid features a unique arrangement of the numbers one to nine. This arrangement is deemed to be magical because the sum of three numbers in any direction in the square – horizontally, vertically, or diagonally – is 15, the number of days taken for a new moon to reach full moon. The Lo Shu square is, therefore, particularly significant in the

time dimension of feng shui, supplementing the space dimension of general feng shui practice.

The three-grid pattern corresponds to the eight sides of the Pa Kua symbol, around a ninth central point. Like the Pa Kua, the direction south is placed at the top so that the number nine also corresponds to the direction south. The pattern of numbers is thus associated with the eight trigrams of the Pa Kua symbol when it is configured according to the Later Heaven Arrangement.

Feng shui practice bases many of its recommendations on the interpretation of

THE MAGIC SQUARE

Add up the numbers on the Lo Shu square in any direction and the result is always fifteen.

~26~

the relationships between the numbers of the Lo Shu square and the symbols of the Pa Kua. These emblems, therefore, exert a powerful and almost mythical influence on all aspects of Chinese cultural symbolism and their various attributes make up much of the underlying basis of feng shui practice today. This is because veteran practitioners in Taiwan, Hong Kong, Singapore, Malaysia, and elsewhere have discovered that the potency of these symbols remains undiminished when correctly applied to the orientation and architecture of modern buildings, towns, and cities.

The Lo Shu square of magic numbers superimposed on the back of the turtle – one of the four celestial animals.

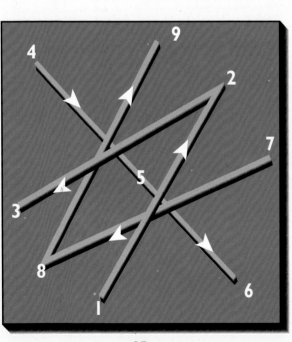

There are striking similarities between the sequence of numbers on the Lo Shu square and symbols from other cultures, especially the Hebrew sign for the planet Saturn.

THE TOOLS OF FENG SHUI PRACTICE

DEMYSTIFYING THE LUO PAN COMPASS

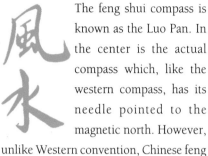

The feng shui compass is known as the Luo Pan. In the center is the actual compass which, like the western compass, has its needle pointed to the magnetic north. However, unlike Western convention, Chinese feng shui practitioners make their analysis using south as the benchmark.

Ancient texts on the subject place south at the top and feng shui symbols also correspond to south being at the top. In practice however, the Chinese direction south is exactly the same as the south referred to by people in the West. Similarly, the Chinese direction north is exactly the same magnetic north used in the West. It is thus not necessary to use a Chinese feng shui Luo Pan. Any good Western compass is perfectly adequate. Equally, it is not necessary to transpose the directions. Whether you live in the northern or southern hemisphere, and whether you live in the East or the West, all directions referred to are the actual, real directions as indicated by an ordinary, modern compass.

The Luo Pan is a reference tool used by feng shui masters, and veterans of the science usually have their own versions of the Luo Pan containing summaries of their own notes and interpretations. These notes are jealously guarded as trade secrets and are placed in code in concentric rings around the compass. As the rings get larger, the meanings get deeper and refer to more advanced formulas. It is sufficient for the amateur practitioner to understand the

Any western compass can be used instead of the Luo Pan.

The first few rings of the Luo Pan show the relationship between the different symbols employed in feng shui practice.

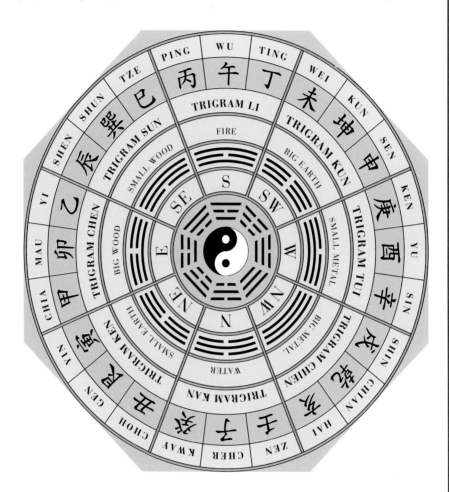

first few inner rings of the compass and their meanings are illustrated here for easy reference.

When studying the feng shui compass, note that advanced feng shui uses secret formulas that examine the directions of doors, the flow of water, and the orientation of houses. These formulas divide each of the eight directions into three sub-directions, thereby offering different recommendations for each of 24 possible directions. Formula feng shui requires very precise and careful measurements of compass directions.

THE CHINESE CALENDAR

An important aspect of feng shui practice uses a person's date of birth and ruling year elements to determine the suitability of directions for doors and orientation for sleeping and working. Use the calendar here to convert Western birth dates into the equivalent Chinese dates for later analysis of Kua numbers. Take note of your birth year element, as this lets you know which elements will be auspicious for you.

Year	From	To	Element	Year	From	To	Element
1900	31 Jan 1900	18 Feb 1901	Metal	1923	16 Feb 1923	4 Feb 1924	Water
1901	19 Feb 1901	17 Feb 1902	Metal	1924	5 Feb 1924	24 Jan 1925	Wood
1902	8 Feb 1902	28 Jan 1903	Water	1925	25 Jan 1925	12 Feb 1926	Wood
1903	29 Jan 1903	15 Jan 1904	Water	1926	13 Feb 1926	1 Feb 1927	Fire
1904	16 Feb 1904	3 Feb 1905	Wood	1927	2 Feb 1927	22 Jan 1928	Fire
1905	4 Feb 1905	24 Jan1906	Wood	1928	23 Jan 1928	9 Feb 1929	Earth
1906	25 Jan 1906	12 Feb 1907	Fire	1929	10 Feb 1929	29 Jan 1930	Earth
1907	13 Feb 1907	1 Feb 1908	Fire	1930	30 Jan 1930	16 Feb 1931	Metal
1908	2 Feb 1908	21 Jan 1909	Earth	1931	17 Feb 1931	15 Feb 1932	Metal
1909	22 Jan 1909	9 Feb 1910	Earth	1932	6 Feb 1932	25 Jan 1933	Water
1910	10 Feb 1910	29 Jan 1911	Metal	1933	26 Jan 1933	13 Feb 1934	Water
1911	30 Jan 1911	17 Feb 1912	Metal	1934	14 Feb 1934	3 Feb 1935	Wood
1912	18 Feb 1912	25 Feb 1913	Water	1935	4 Feb 1935	23 Jan 1936	Wood
1913	6 Feb 1913	25 Jan 1914	Water	1936	24 Jan 1936	10 Feb 1937	Fire
1914	26 Jan 1914	13 Feb 1915	Wood	1937	11 Feb 1937	30 Jan 1938	Fire
1915	14 Feb 1915	2 Feb 1916	Wood	1938	31 Jan 1938	18 Feby 1939	Earth
1916	3 Feb 1916	22 Jan 1917	Fire	1939	19 Feb 1939	7 Feb 1940	Earth
1917	23 Jan 1917	10 Feb 1918	Fire	1940	8 Feb 1940	26 Jan 1941	Metal
1918	11 Feb 1918	31 Jan 1919	Earth	1941	27 Jan 1941	14 Feb 1942	Metal
1919	1 Feb 1919	19 Feb 1920	Earth	1942	15 Feb 1942	24 Feb 1943	Water
1920	20 Feb 1920	7 Feb 1921	Metal	1943	5 Feb 1943	24 Jan 1944	Water
1921	8 Feb 1921	27 Jan 1922	Metal	1944	25 Jan 1944	12 Feb 1945	Wood
1922	28 Jan 1922	15 Feb 1923	Water	1945	13 Feb 1945	1 Feb 1946	Wood

Year	From	To	Element	Year	From	To	Element
1946	2 Feb 1946	21 Jan 1947	Fire	1977	18 Feb 1977	6 Feb 1978	Fire
1947	22 Jan 1947	9 Feb 1948	Fire	1978	7 Feb 1978	27 Jan 1979	Earth
1948	10 Feb 1948	28 Jan 1949	Earth	1979	28 Jan 1979	15 Feb 1980	Earth
1949	29 Jan 1949	16 Feb 1950	Earth	1980	16 Feb 1980	4 Feb 1981	Metal
1950	17 Feb 1950	5 Feb 1951	Metal	1981	5 Feb 1981	24 Jan 1982	Metal
1951	6 Feb 1951	26 Jan 1952	Metal	1982	25 Jan 1982	12 Feb 1983	Water
1952	27 Jan 1952	13 Feb 1953	Water	1983	13 Feb 1983	1 Feb 1984	Water
1953	14 Feb 1953	2 Feb 1954	Water	1984	2 Feb 1984	19 Feb 1985	Wood
1954	3 Feb 1954	23 Jan 1955	Wood	1985	20 Feb 1985	8 Feb 1986	Wood
1955	24 Jan 1955	11 Feb 1956	Wood	1986	9 Feb 1986	28 Jan 1987	Fire
1956	12 Feb 1956	30 Jan 1957	Fire	1987	29 Jan 1987	16 Feb 1988	Fire
1957	31 Jan 1957	17 Feb 1958	Fire	1988	17 Feb 1988	5 Feb 1989	Earth
1958	18 Feb 1958	7 Feb 1959	Earth	1989	6 Feb 1989	26 Jan 1990	Earth
1959	8 Feb 1959	27 Jan 1960	Earth	1990	27 Jan 1990	14 Feb 1991	Metal
1960	28 Jan 1960	14 Feb 1961	Metal	1991	15 Feb 1991	3 Feb 1992	Metal
1961	15 Feb 1961	4 Feb 1962	Metal	1992	4 Feb 1992	22 Jan 1993	Water
1962	5 Feb 1962	24 Jan 1963	Water	1993	23 Jan 1993	9 Feb 1994	Water
1963	25 Jan 1963	12 Feb 1964	Water	1994	10 Feb 1994	30 Jan 1995	Wood
1964	13 Feb 1964	1 Feb 1965	Wood	1995	31 Jan 1995	18 Feb 1996	Wood
1965	2 Feb 1965	20 Jan 1966	Wood	1996	19 Feb 1996	7 Feb 1997	Fire
1966	21 Jan 1966	8 Feb 1967	Fire	1997	8 Feb 1997	27 Jan 1998	Fire
1967	9 Feb 1967	29 Jan 1968	Fire	1998	28 Jan 1998	15 Feb 1999	Earth
1968	30 Jan 1968	16 Feb 1969	Earth	1999	16 Feb 1999	4 Feb 2000	Earth
1969	17 Feb 1969	5 Feb 1970	Earth	2000	5 Feb 2000	23 Jan 2001	Metal
1970	6 Feb 1970	26 Jan 1971	Metal	2001	24 Jan 2001	11 Feb 2002	Metal
1971	27 Jan 1971	15 Feb 1972	Metal	2002	12 Feb 2002	31 Jan 2003	Water
1972	16 Feb 1972	22 Feb 1973	Water	2003	1 Feb 2003	21 Jan 2004	Water
1973	3 Feb 1973	22 Jan 1974	Water	2004	22 Jan 2004	8 Feb 2005	Wood
1974	23 Jan 1974	10 Feb 1975	Wood	2005	9 Feb 2005	28 Jan 2006	Wood
1975	11 Feb 1975	30 Jan 1976	Wood	2006	29 Jan 2006	17 Feb 2007	Fire
1976	31 Jan 1976	17 Feb 1977	Fire	2007	18 Feb 2007	6 Feb 2008	Fire

0mm

50

100

150

200

250

300

350

400

CHAI

YI

KWAN

PUN

THE FENG SHUI RULER

There are auspicious and inauspicious dimensions and most Chinese carpenters possess something called the feng shui ruler, which allows them to see at a glance whether the tables, closets, windows, and doors that they are making have acceptable dimensions.

The feng shui measuring tape has eight cycles of dimensions, four of which are auspicious and four inauspicious. Each cycle measures the equivalent of

AUSPICIOUS DIMENSIONS

CHAI: this is the first segment of the cycle and is subdivided into four categories of good luck, each approximately 1/2in or 13mm. The first brings money luck, the second brings a safe filled with jewels, the third brings together six types of good luck, while the fourth brings abundance. (Chai: 0–2⅛ins, 0–54mm.)

YI: this is the fourth segment of the cycle. It brings mentor luck, that is, it attracts helpful people into your life. The first sub-section means luck with children, the second predicts unexpected added income, the third predicts a very successful son, and the fourth offers good fortune. (Yi: 6⅜–8½ins, 162–215mm.)

KWAN: this third set of auspicious dimensions bring power luck and is similarly divided into four sub-sections. The first sub-sector means ease in passing exams, the second predicts special or speculative luck, the third offers improved income, while the fourth attracts high honors for the family. (Kwan: 8½–10⅝ins, 215–270mm.)

PUN: this fourth set of auspicious dimensions is divided into four sub-sections like the others. The first sub-sector bring lots of money flowing in, the next spells good luck in examinations, the third predicts plenty of jewelry, and the fourth sub-sector offers abundant prosperity. (Pun: 14¾in–17ins, 375–432mm.)

17 inches or 432mm, and each cycle is categorized into eight sections. The cycle of lucky and unlucky dimensions then repeats itself continuously. Once you have familiarized yourself with the use of the feng shui ruler, you can apply it to almost everything measurable to tap into the auspicious dimensions. In addition to furniture, doors, and windows, you can also use it on calling cards, envelopes, notepads or memo paper.

INAUSPICIOUS DIMENSIONS

PI: this category of bad luck refers to sickness. It also has four sub-sectors, each approximately $\frac{1}{2}$in or 13mm. The first carries the meaning money retreats, the second indicates legal problems, the third means bad luck – even going to jail – and the fourth indicates death of a spouse. (Pi: $2\frac{1}{8}$–$4\frac{1}{4}$ins, 54–108mm.)

LI: this category means separation and is similarly divided into four sub-sections. The first means a store of bad luck, the second predicts losing money, the third says you will meet up with unscrupulous people, and the fourth predicts being a victim of theft or burglary. (Li: $4\frac{1}{4}$–$6\frac{3}{8}$ins, 108–162mm.)

CHIEH: this category of bad dimension spells loss and has four sub-sections. The first spells death or departure of some kind, the second that everything you need will disappear and you could lose your livelihood, the third indicates you will be chased out of your village in disgrace, and the fourth indicates a very severe loss of money. (Chieh: $10\frac{5}{8}$–$12\frac{3}{4}$ins, 270–324mm.)

HAI: this fourth set of inauspicious dimensions indicates severe bad luck, starting with disasters arriving in the first sub-sector, death in the second, sicknesses and ill health in the third, and scandal and quarrels in the fourth. (Hai: $12\frac{3}{4}$–$14\frac{3}{4}$ins, 324–375mm.)

0mm
50
PI
100
LI
150
200
250
CHIEH
300
350
HAI
400

FORM SCHOOL
FENG SHUI

CONFIGURATION OF THE LANDSCAPE

 The form school focuses on the configurations of the landscape, the presence of mountains and hills, waterways and lakes, the quality of the soil, and the wind, as well as the shapes and sizes of surrounding structures. Practicing landscape feng shui requires an understanding of animal symbolism because types of elevations are described as dragon or tiger hills or as turtle mountains and phoenix footstools. Elevations are also described in terms of the five elements (wood, fire, water, metal, and earth). Classical descriptions of good feng shui configurations have the mountain behind, preferably located north, the phoenix in front, preferably placed south and the dragon and the tiger curled in the form of an armchair.

If your home is surrounded by hills in this manner, your family will be rich for generations. The dragon brings prosperity, the tiger protects you, the turtle assures you of longevity, and the phoenix brings you great opportunities. If there is also a river running in front of you, in full view of your front door, and it flows from left to right, you will be guaranteed enormous success in everything you undertake.

TOWNS AND CITIES

Hills and mountains can refer to buildings, and roads can take the place of rivers in town and city dwellers' analyses. Always ensure the following.

- ▨ Your main front door is not blocked by a large or tall building.
- ▨ The back of your building is protected by a taller or larger structure or hills in the distance.
- ▨ Buildings or raised ground on the left of your main door (looking out from inside) are higher than land on the right. The tiger must never be higher, otherwise it turns malevolent. If it is, install a bright spotlight high up on the left side of your main door.

THE TWO SCHOOLS

There are two major schools of feng shui practice. The form school looks at feng shui visually, diagnosing balance in terms of shape and form of the terrain. The compass school (see pages 34–39) takes a more precise view of orientation and direction and uses the compass extensively. Both schools are equally important and both methods should be used to get the best out of feng shui.

This house is situated where the hills to the right, the white tiger hills, are higher than those on the left, the green dragon hills. When the tiger is higher than the dragon it becomes malevolent rather than protective. However, its negative influences can be deflected by installing a very bright spotlight high up to the left of the front door.

GREEN DRAGONS, WHITE TIGERS, AND THE COSMIC BREATH

Classical feng shui talks about the green dragon and the white tiger, two of the four celestial animals used in landscape symbolism to assist practitioners to search out land sites that promise good luck. Dragons are never found where land is completely flat or where there are only jagged mountains – and where there is no dragon, the tiger, too, will be missing. Such locations are said to be extremely inauspicious.

Dragons and tigers are found where the land is gently undulating, the vegetation looks healthy and lush, the breezes are mild, the soil looks fertile, and the sunlight and shade are in balance. Such locations are extremely auspicious, but they are difficult to identify. A formation of hills alone seldom offers clear enough indications and different types of high ground often exist side by side, making the search even harder. There are, however, some useful clues that you can look out for.

- Look for cloistered corners where the vegetation seems extra verdant.
- Feel the breeze and smell the air. If the wind is gentle and the air smells good, the dragon lives nearby.
- Look for places where there is both sunlight and shade.
- Dragons do not live on hilltops, where there is little protection. Avoid such sites.
- Dragons are not found where overhanging ridges and rocky outcrops threaten from above.
- Avoid land that is rocky and hard.
- Damp and musty places do not house dragons.

The dragon is always accompanied by the tiger. Identify them by seeing how the range of hills curves. Where two ranges meet, as if in an embrace, the site is deemed to be very special. This is where the dragon and the tiger are said to exude the greatest amount of cosmic breath, the sheng chi which brings extreme good fortune.

ENERGIZING THE CELESTIAL ANIMALS

The guidelines of dragon and tiger symbolism in landscape feng shui can be simulated indoors very simply. Place a painting or ceramic model of a dragon against the east wall of your living room to energize the auspicious dragon. Let your main entrance door open into a small hall so that when the chi enters it has a chance to settle and not just rush away. Place turtles – real terrapins in an aquarium or ceramic models – in the north corner of your living room or behind your desk to symbolize the strong support of this celestial creature. Hang a picture of a glowing red phoenix in the south corner to bring opportunities your way.

The image of a dragon on the east wall of a room attracts the auspicious energy associated with this celestial animal.

The main premise of feng shui is to capture the auspicious chi of the dragon. Different parts of the dragon emit different quantities of chi, and feng shui is concerned with locating places in the landscape where it accumulates in abundance. These are areas that represent the dragon's heart and belly. The extremities of its body, such as the tail, are areas of stagnant chi. So a house built at the edge of elevated land, or on completely flat, low-lying land, will suffer from unsettled circumstances. There is no stability where the chi is tired.

Locations where the cosmic breath is scattered by high winds or carried away by fast-flowing rivers have no feng shui potential. Good luck cannot accumulate as chi evaporates before it can settle. A site is only auspicious when the flow of chi accumulates. Look for the following.

- Places where there are slow, meandering rivers.
- Places that are bordered by water.
- Places that are protected against harsh winds.
- Places where the surrounding hills are not too sharply pointed.

HILLS AND WATERCOURSES

There is also element significance in hills and watercourses. Their shapes and configurations, the way hills rise, and the way waters flow offer indications of their intrinsic element. Thus, there are water hills and fire waters and, depending on the ruling element of your year of birth, you can measure the degree of your personal affinity with the natural land forms and water that surround your own home.

TYPES OF HILL

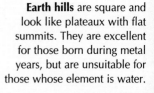

Fire hills are conical in shape, rising up boldly, straight to a keen-edged, sharp point. Metal element people should not live near such hills, but those born in an earth year would benefit. However, this kind of hill directly facing the main door is disastrous for everyone.

Wood hills are round. They rise straight, have a long body, and are round at the summit. Those born in fire years are especially suited to living near such hills, but earth year people should avoid them. These hills are auspicious when they are behind the house.

Earth hills are square and look like plateaux with flat summits. They are excellent for those born during metal years, but are unsuitable for those whose element is water.

Water hills are ridged and appear to have several summits so that they look like a continuous range. Fire year people should not live near them, but wood element people will benefit from the affinity of energies with such a hill range.

Metal hills are oblong and are softly rounded, with a broad base and gentle slopes. These are suitable for those born during water years and are inauspicious for those born in wood years.

Wood

Water

Metal

Fire

Earth

INAUSPICIOUS SHAPES

Shapes that attract ill fortune are triangular, incomplete, and irregular. Other unlucky shapes are L- or U-shaped land and houses. Shapes that seem to have bits and pieces missing or jutting out are also deemed to be unbalanced and bring various different kinds of misfortunes, depending on which corners are missing and which jut out.

Missing corners can often be corrected by installing mirrors on walls, as these visually extend the corner. Alternatively, you can install a high, bright light in the missing corner which will serve to extend it symbolically.

Protruding corners appear like extensions to the basic shape with the result that other corners seem to be lacking. Since every corner of the home represents some kind of good fortune, these extensions can be auspicious or inauspicious depending on whether they are located in your personalized direction.

SHAPES

A selection of inauspicious shapes are shown here.

Regular shapes are always preferred to irregular shapes. So, for the purposes of feng shui, perfectly square or rectangular shapes are always deemed luckier than odd shapes. This is true for plots of land, houses, other buildings, rooms, windows, doors, and tables. Regular shapes are symmetrical and balanced; nothing is missing. For the practice of more advanced feng shui, which offers wonderful suggestions for energizing the various corners of a room or home, maximum benefit can be gained only when working with regular-shaped rooms. It is also easier to superimpose the Pa Kua and the Lo Shu square onto a regular-shaped room for additional feng shui analysis.

THE FLOW OF WATER

The angles made by flowing water are also described in terms of the five elements. If you live near a waterway or have drains around your home, check the suitability of the angles in relation to your personal year element, as well as to the element represented by the angle of the water. For example, angles in the north should ideally be of the water or metal element, in the south, of the fire or wood element and so forth.

COMPASS SCHOOL FENG SHUI

USING FORMULAS

Compass feng shui offers very precise use of formulas that spell out specific ways of investigating auspicious or inauspicious directions for orienting doors and entrances, the placement of furniture, and the direction for sleeping.

There are formulas to calculate individual auspicious and inauspicious directions based on personal Kua numbers and others for working out lucky and unlucky sectors of buildings from month to month and from year to year. The formulas address both the space and time dimensions of feng shui. They differentiate between east and west groups of people and buildings, offering methods for balancing personal energies with those of the environment. There are also formulas that address specific types of luck, particularly wealth luck, that have to do with the correct placement of water and its direction of flow around the living area.

Compass formula feng shui is a little more complex to learn than form school feng shui. However it is less subjective, which makes it easier to practice. Two of the formulas used in compass feng shui are given here.

AUSPICIOUS AND INAUSPICIOUS DIRECTIONS

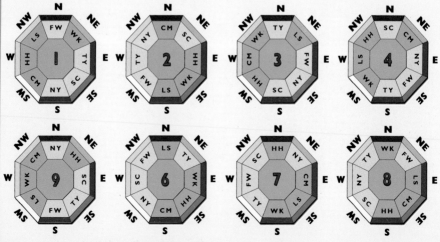

THE KUA NUMBERS FORMULA

This is a powerfully potent method for discovering personalized auspicious and inauspicious directions based on birth dates. Calculate your Kua number as follows:

Check against the Chinese calendar (see pages 24-25) to make sure you use your Chinese year of birth.

Males

- Take your year of birth.
- Add the last two digits.
- If the result is more than 10, add the two digits to reduce them to a single number.
- Subtract from **10**.
- **The answer is your Kua number.**

Example year of birth 1936:
3+6=9;
10-9=1
The Kua is **1**.

Females

- Take your year of birth.
- Add the last two digits.
- If the result is more than 10, add the two digits to reduce them to a single number.
- Add **5**.
- The answer is your Kua number.

Example year of birth 1945:
4+5=9;
9+5-14;
1+4=5
The Kua is **5**.

The Kua numbers are the key to unlocking your auspicious and inauspicious directions. Kua numbers one, three, four, and nine have east, southeast, north, and south as the auspicious directions. The specific ranking of each of these directions and the precise type of luck they activate for you make up the more detailed aspects of this formula and differ for each of the Kua numbers. It is sufficient to know that with these Kua numbers you are an east group person. The inauspicious directions for you are, therefore, the other four, the west group directions.

Kua numbers two, six, seven, and eight have west, southwest, northwest, and northeast as the auspicious directions. Again the specific ranking of each of these directions differs for each of the Kua numbers, but these are west group directions. The inauspicious directions for you are thus the other four, east group directions. There is no Kua number 5 in this system. Males who have a Kua number of 5 should use the number 2 and females who have a Kua number of 5 should use the number 8.

Auspicious Locations	Inauspicious Locations
Fu Wei = FW	Ho Hai = HH
Tien Yi =TY	Wu Kwei =WK
Nien Yen=NY	Chueh Ming=CM
Sheng Chi=SC	Lui Sha=LS

When using formula feng shui it is essential to be very accurate in your measurements and also when taking compass directions. Note the elements that are represented in each of the directions.

APPLYING THE KUA FORMULA

The home should be demarcated into the nine sectors according to the Lo Shu grid as shown. To do this accurately, use a good measuring tape and try to get the demarcations as accurate as possible.

Next, get your bearings and identify the eight corners according to their compass directions. Please note that although feng shui books usually place south at the top according to Chinese tradition, the actual directions referred to are identical with those used in the West. Thus the Chinese north is exactly the same as the north indicated by any Western-style compass. So you can use a good Western compass and, standing in the center of your home, identify the eight side locations by dividing the floor space of the home into a grid of nine equal squares. Draw out the floor plan of your home, as this will assist in the arrangement of rooms and furniture.

BIG METAL

Northwest

SMALL METAL

West

BIG EARTH

Southwest

Even as you identify the sectors, keep the matching elements of each compass location at the back of your mind. This is because the application of the five element theory transcends every school of feng shui, and irrespective of the method or formula being used, it is necessary to remember this. For ease of reference, the elements are indicated in each of the sectors. This is according to the Later Heaven Arrangement of the trigrams, the arrangement always used for the living. The element of the center is earth.

Please note that rooms do not necessarily all fit neatly into the Lo Shu grid. Most rooms fall within two or even three sectors. This is when the exact placement of important pieces of furniture, such as desks and beds, in the room becomes extremely important.

WATER

North

EARTH

Northeast

BIG WOOD

East

FIRE

South

SMALL WOOD

Southeast

IMPLEMENTING
YOUR KUA NUMBER

Follow these suggestions for using Kua numbers for auspicious directions.

▧ Orientate your main door to face one of your auspicious directions.

▧ Work at a desk facing one of your auspicious directions.

▧ Sleep with your head pointing at one of your good directions.

▧ Eat, negotiate, give lectures, in other words undertake most activities, facing one of your best directions.

▧ Try to avoid having to do any of the above facing any of your inauspicious directions.

Orientate your door to face one of your best directions.

EXAMPLE

If your Kua number is **four**, you are an east group person and your auspicious directions are east, southeast, north, and south. These are the directions that you should face for your main and most important activities, as shown in the illustration here.

Always calculate the direction in which you should face by standing in the middle of the room and looking outward.

Select the seat in a meeting room or at the dining table at home that allows you to face one of your auspicious directions.

Sleep with your head pointing toward one of your best directions.

~ 45 ~

IRREGULAR-SHAPED HOMES

Houses, apartments, and offices rarely have regular, square, or rectangular shapes, making it difficult to superimpose a nine-sector grid onto the layout. More serious is the problem of missing corners. There are ways of getting round this problem and some common problems, together with solutions, are shown here.

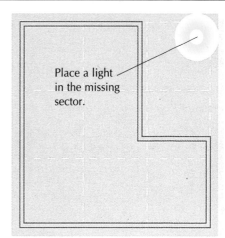

Place a light in the missing sector.

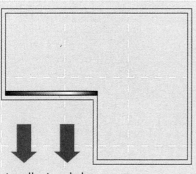

A wall mirror helps offset the problem of irregularly-shaped rooms.

▓ Install a light.
▓ Hang a wall mirror.
▓ Build an extension.

What you do depends on your circumstances and whether you have the necessary space available.

An irregular-shaped layout sometimes makes it difficult to have the main door located in, or oriented in, the most

The examples shown are homes with irregular layout shapes. According to feng shui, missing corners mean the home will be lacking in certain luck aspects. What type of luck is missing depends on the corresponding compass direction of the missing sector.

If one missing sector represents your success direction, you can partially correct the matter by one of the three methods shown on this page.

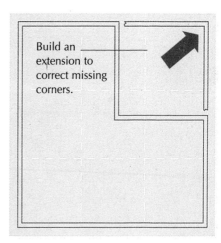

Build an extension to correct missing corners.

auspicious way. If you cannot put your door in this location, tapping the success direction alone is often good enough. If you cannot tap either the location or direction, try at least to have your main door face one of your four auspicious directions. Remember that directions are taken inside the home facing outward.

EAST AND WEST GROUP DIRECTIONS

Compass feng shui divides people into east and west groups. Your other auspicious directions depend on whether you are an east or a west group person. This is based on your Kua number.

East group people have Kua numbers one, three, four, and nine. East group directions are east, north, south, and southeast. West group people have Kua numbers two, five, six, seven, and eight. West group directions are west, southwest, northwest, and northeast.

East group directions are detrimental to west group people and vice versa. Try at all costs to have your main entrance face one of your group's auspicious directions.

ALLOCATING ROOMS ACCORDING TO THE TRIGRAMS

To get the best out of feng shui, allocate rooms to family members taking your cue from the trigrams around the Pa Kua of the Later Heaven Arrangement. This is appropriate for yang dwellings – the homes of the living as opposed to yin dwellings – homes for the dead.

The method of superimposing the nine-sector Lo Shu grid which divides the home into nine sectors, is described on pages 42–43, after which the directions should be taken with a compass.

ROOMS FOR THE FAMILY

According to the Pa Kua of the Later Heaven Arrangement, the eight directions of any living space that correspond to the eight directions of the compass are as follows:

- ▨ The northwest for the father.
- ▨ The southwest for the mother.
- ▨ The east for the eldest or only son.
- ▨ The southeast for the eldest or only daughter.
- ▨ The north for the middle son.
- ▨ The south for the middle daughter.
- ▨ The northeast for the youngest son.
- ▨ The west for the youngest daughter.

ROOMS FOR PARENTS

The parents, especially the father, can be located in the northwest because the trigram for this direction is Chien, which represents the father. Practitioners of feng shui can choose to locate the master bedroom according to this method or they can follow the compass formula, which offers personal best directions based on the date of birth (see page 41). The method used is often dependent on the home itself, as there is not always complete freedom of choice due to constraints of shape and space.

The southwest is represented by the trigram Kun, which signifies the matriarch. This direction would be well suited to house the family room, since the female maternal spirit cares for the welfare of the entire family.

ROOMS FOR CHILDREN

Ideally, the sons of the family should sleep in the room that corresponds to the east of the home. If there is more than one son, other suitable rooms for them are the north and northeast. The east is, however, the best place for all the sons of the family since the trigram here is Chen, which means successful growth.

The daughters of the family can be located with equal advantage in the southeast, the south, or the west. The favorite daughter (usually the youngest) is usually the one who sleeps in the west, since the trigram here is Tui, which means joyous and it also symbolizes young women.

Allocating rooms according to the trigrams of the Later Heaven Arrangement will ensure beneficial feng shui for the family.

Father in the northwest

Sons in the northeast or east

Mother in the southwest

Daughter in the southeast

THE EIGHT LIFE ASPIRATIONS FORMULA

This formula is based on interpretations of the eight trigrams that are placed round the Later Heaven Pa Kua and is one of the easier compass theories to apply. Each side of the Pa Kua corresponds to a particular direction and is deemed to represent a specific kind of luck. Eight types of luck are identified and these are said to correspond to the sum total of humankind's aspirations. You will find, as you go deeper into feng shui, that the Chinese concept of luck is always expressed in terms of these particular eight aspirations.

▓ The attainment of wealth and prosperity.

▓ The attainment of a happy marriage.

▓ Getting respect, honor, and recognition.

▓ Longevity and good health.

▓ Having good descendants, that is, children and, specifically, sons.

▓ The attainment of education and knowledge.

▓ The help and support of influential people.

▓ Career promotions.

These aspirations can be specifically energized in several different ways that combine the use of other feng shui methods and formulas. Each of these eight types of luck is discussed in more comprehensive detail in the other books in this series. As an introduction to the method, however, it is useful to study the illustrated Pa Kua here that provides the basic formula.

Sun
South-east
Wealth and prosperity

Chen
East
Family relationships and health

Ken
North-east
Education

Li

South

Recognition and fame

Kun

South-west

Marriage prospects and marital happiness

Tui

West

Luck of children

Kan

North

Career prospects

Chien

North-west

Presence of helpful people or mentors

POISON ARROWS AND THE KILLING BREATH

THE KILLING BREATH

Bad feng shui is almost always caused by what is termed the killing breath, or shar chi, and every school of feng shui repeatedly warns against being hit by the shar chi of secret poison arrows within the environment that bring this deadly and pernicious energy. These usually come in the form of straight lines, sharp angles, or anything that is shaped this way. When pointed in a threatening manner at your home, especially at your front door, the result is extreme bad luck, loss, and ill health. In some cases the poison arrows can even bring death to the unfortunate residents of the house.

When practicing feng shui it is advisable to start by taking a defensive posture to guard against the killing breath. Only then should you turn your attention to harnessing good chi flows. Remember that, even if you have the best dragon and tiger configurations and irrespective of all your orientations being auspicious, a single deadly arrow can spoil everything.

The straight lines of this row of poplar trees can, in some situations, act like poison arrows directing the killing breath toward your home.

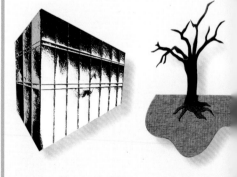

OTHER EXAMPLE

Sharp edge of a building   A dead tree trur

POISON ARROWS

Poison arrows that cause shar chi can be any hostile, threatening, or imposing structure whose energies overwhelm the energies of your home. They can also be straight hill ridges, the angle of a roof line, the edge of a building, or a straight road or river.

THE T-JUNCTION

If the front door of your house faces a T-junction, as shown here, or any other offending structure, you can protect yourself against the killing breath in one of several ways.

▨ Re-orientate or move your main door so that the bad energy is deflected.

▨ Plant a row of trees with good foliage so that the oncoming road is 'blocked off'.

▨ Build a wall that effectively closes off the view of the offending road.

▨ Hang a Pa Kua with a mirror outside above the center of the door to ward off the shar chi and prevent it from entering your home.

F POISON ARROWS

Any kind of tower

A mirror will deflect shar chi away from your home

LOOKING OUT FOR ARROWS

Unless you deliberately become aware of your surroundings, it is easy to miss hostile structures that could well be sending harmful energies your way. Looking out for poison arrows requires practice. Just remember that anything sharp, pointed, angular, or hostile has the potential to harm you if it is directed toward your door.

- ▨ A common cause of shar chi is the triangular shape of the roof lines of a neighbor's house. If such a structure is facing you, try to re-orient your door.
- ▨ Living near to or facing electrical transmitters or pylons often causes negative energies to build up. Shield them from view by growing a clump of trees between them and your home.

- ▨ Directly facing a church, any kind of steeple, or a huge cross is inauspicious. Reflect back any negative vibrations with a Pa Kua mirror.

Other examples of structures that can emanate poisonous or killing breath at your home include signboards and pointers, windmills, sharp hills, tall buildings, cannons, and tree trunks. Remember that they are harmful from a feng shui viewpoint only if they are directly hitting, or facing, the main front door of your house.

- ▨ A highway overpass that resembles blades hitting the front of your home also causes imbalance. Move away from such a house or building or hang a large wind chime between the overpass and your door.

Certain features in your surroundings, like sharp mountains (right), have the potential to create problems for you if their harmful energies are pointed directly at your main front door.

OBJECTS CAN DEFLECT POISON ARROWS

When dealing with poison arrows, try to match the element of the object used as a cure with the compass location where there is a problem. Listed here are six such objects that can be used to deal with poison arrows.

WIND CHIMES

They are often excellent for countering the ill effects of protrusions from ceilings and structural beams. Metal wind chimes are especially effective when they are hung in the west and northwest corners of rooms.

PLANTS

These are excellent for shielding and dissolving shar chi, especially when placed against corners. As they also symbolize growth, they are perfect feng shui when placed in the east corners of rooms.

SCREENS

These are extremely popular with the Chinese as they are good at blocking energy that is moving too fast. By slowing down the pernicious breath, screens transform harmful energy into auspicious energy.

DRAPES

These are very effective when used to block out bad views of threatening structures that create shar chi. Use heavy drapes or chintz curtains. They are effective in any corner of the home, but select colors according to the elements of the corners. Use red for the south, dark blue for the north, green for the east, and white for the west.

MIRRORS

These are powerful feng shui tools because their reflective quality has the effect of sending shar chi to back where it came from. Mirrors also widen narrow, cramped corners and extend walls to make up for missing corners. However, they should be used carefully. They must not reflect the main door, nor should they reflect toilets. Mirrors are auspicious in dining rooms but should not reflect the bed of the master bedroom.

LIGHTS

These are powerful antidotes for all kinds of feng shui problems. They are especially good when used to dissolve the shar chi of sharp edges and protruding corners, particularly when placed in the south corners of rooms, except angular lights like this which are not beneficial.

DEALING WITH
ARROWS INSIDE THE HOME

It is also necessary to watch out for poison arrows inside the home. Shar chi is usually created when there are sharp edges caused by furniture, protruding corners, individual square pillars, and exposed overhead beams. Being hit by the sharp edges of these structures causes migraine and other illnesses and, in severe cases, it can also bring bad luck in the form of unexpected financial and career loss.

Block off the sharp edge of a protruding corner with a large plant as shown here.

Dissolve the shar chi of individual square pillars by covering them with mirrors that effectively make them disappear.

Placing crystals at the edge of a sharp protruding corner will deflect shar chi.

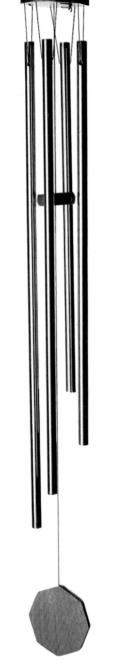

Deal with exposed overhead beams
by hanging two flutes, tied with red
thread and positioned diagonally.

Alternatively, hang a wind chime
to soften the shar chi emanating
from a beam.

Open book shelves are bad feng shui.
They act like blades, cutting at residents.
It is always preferable to have doors.

FENG SHUI TIPS FOR INTERIORS

RESIDENTIAL ROOM LAYOUTS

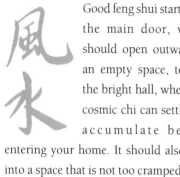

Good feng shui starts with the main door, which should open outward to an empty space, termed the bright hall, where the cosmic chi can settle and accumulate before entering your home. It should also lead into a space that is not too cramped. This allows chi to gather before meandering through your home.

MAIN DOOR TABOOS

- ❋ The main door should never open into a cramped hall. Install a bright light if the space is too narrow.
- ❋ The main door should never open directly into a staircase. Place a screen in between or curve the bottom of the stairs.
- ❋ There should not be a toilet too near the main door. This causes chi that enters the home to become sour.

Well-lit and clean apartments attract auspicious energies. Small, dark, and unused corners create killing breath, so air store rooms occasionally. Do not have too many doors opening from a long corridor; this will cause quarrels. The ratio of windows to doors should not exceed 3:1. Doors should not directly face a window, as chi will come in and go out again.

THREE DOORS

Three doors in a straight line are deadly feng shui. The chi is moving too fast. Hang a wind chime or place a dividing screen in front of the middle door.

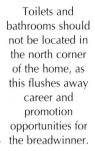

Toilets and bathrooms should not be located in the north corner of the home, as this flushes away career and promotion opportunities for the breadwinner.

Staircases should ideally be curved and winding. Spiral staircases resemble a corkscrew and are harmless when placed in a corner, but deadly when located in the middle of the home.

Rooms should be regular in shape, with kitchens located in the back half of the home.

Dining areas should be higher than living rooms if there are split levels.

The ideal arrangement of rooms will encourage chi to move smoothly through your home.

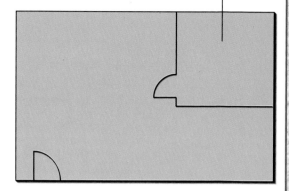

Good room location at the far corner of the office building.

If you take care over the feng shui of your office, your business will prosper.

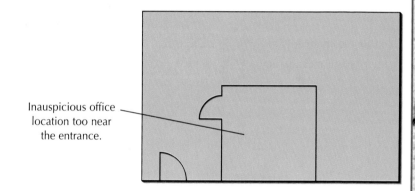

Inauspicious office location too near the entrance.

OFFICE FENG SHUI

When you have good feng shui at work there is harmony in the office and co-operative spirit prevails. Bad feng shui can lead to discord and collapsing profits. If you are in a managerial position, your room should ideally be located deep inside the office, but not at the end of a long corridor. The fortunes of the entire office are affected by your feng shui.

▨ Regular-shaped rooms are always to be preferred over odd-shaped rooms.

▨ All protruding corners should be camouflaged with plants.

▨ Avoid sitting directly below an overhead beam.

▨ If a window opens to a view of a sharp angle, keep it permanently closed.

▨ Do not sit directly facing open book shelves.

SITTING DIRECTIONS

Never sit with your back to the door. You will literally be stabbed in the back. Do not sit with your back to the window. You will lack support for your suggestions and ideas. Always sit facing the door at whatever angle you like and ideally facing one of your good luck directions, according to compass feng shui. Whatever your sitting position and direction, make sure it does not seem awkward. Do not attempt to sit facing your best compass direction if in the process you get stabbed by a poison arrow caused by the arrangement of the office furniture or an individual pillar.

Bad desk placement with the back to the door.

Good desk placement. The desk faces the door. Place a painting or print of a mountain behind the desk to symbolize support.

Never sit too near the door; you will be easily distracted.

ARRANGING FURNITURE

Living room furniture should never be L-shaped. Try to simulate the Pa Kua shape when arranging a lounge suite and coffee table, as this is conducive to creating good social interactions between those sitting there. It is a good idea to find your favorite place when entertaining friends. It should be one of your auspicious compass directions. Place the television and stereo on the west or northwest side and a pot plant or some flowers on the east side of the room. The fireplace should ideally be located in the south, but is also acceptable to situate it in the southwest or northeast.

The television and stereo should ideally be in the west or northwest of the room.

The fireplace should be in the northeast, southwest, or south.

The room where people gather should encourage harmony.

The sofa and armchairs should be arranged in the shape of the Pa Kua.

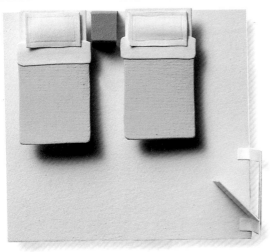

Good bed placement.

Peaceful and
refreshing sleep
will be guaranteed
if the beds are
well placed.

Inauspicious bed
placement.

BEDROOMS

Bedrooms must have good bed arrangements. Place the bed diagonally opposite the door and do not sleep with your feet directly pointed toward it, as this is deemed the death position. Do not sleep under an overhead beam. Do not have mirrors directly facing the bed, as this is extremely inauspicious. While plants generally represent good feng shui, it is not advisable to have them in bedrooms. The yang energy of plants can sometimes disturb the yin energies required for a good night's sleep.

FENG SHUI TIPS
FOR EXTERIORS

CHANNELLING
VIBRANT EARTH ENERGIES

One of the most effective ways of channeling healthy earth energy for the home is to introduce auspicious feng shui features into the garden. No matter how small your garden may be, if the directions are conducive to introducing specific feng shui activators, it is advisable to do so. There are some easy ways of doing this.

- Introduce a garden light if the garden has a south orientation.
- Introduce a small fountain if it has a north orientation.
- Build a low brick wall if it is southwest.

A low brick wall energizes the earth energy of the southwest and northeast, bringing good fortune to the residents.

Garden lights in the south are excellent feng shui.

A fountain or bird bath is great for the north corner of the garden.

Place terrapins in a small trough of water and feed
them regularly or display a fake model of a turtle
above a small mound of earth in your garden.
This should attract good fortune into your home.

Another great way of channeling energy from the ground is to sink a long, hollow pole deep into the ground and place a round light at the top. This encourages auspicious sheng chi to rise and residents enjoy good fortune from this positive energy.

LONGEVITY AND GOOD HEALTH WITH THE TURTLE

Another particularly good tip for the outdoors is to introduce the symbol of longevity in the form of the celestial turtle. Placed in the north part of the garden, real turtles bring exceptionally good luck, but a ceramic model will do just as well. The turtle is symbolic of heavenly luck in the form of good health, protection, and support.

BALANCE IS EVERYTHING

Do not expect overnight success. Be patient and make subtle adjustments when necessary. If you harness and channel earth energy in your home and environment, good fortune will follow.

THE TIME DIMENSION

USING FLYING STAR FENG SHUI

Flying star feng shui is a very popular method used in Hong Kong, Malaysia, and Singapore that addresses the time aspects of feng shui. Flying star adds the vital dynamics of changes brought about by the passage of time, while complementing the space dimension of all other feng shui methods. This is a very advanced method and it is not necessary for amateur practitioners to become too involved in its technical details. However, it is useful to have a reference table to enable you to investigate the impact of flying star on your own feng shui, particularly since this method is excellent for warning against the flying stars that bring illness.

WHAT ARE THE FLYING STARS?

These are the numbers one to nine placed around a nine-sector grid, known as the Lo Shu magic square. The numbers around the grid fly, changing with the passage of time. Every month and year and every 20-year period has its own arrangement of numbers around the square. Every number has its own meanings. For the feng shui expert who knows how to interpret the numbers a great deal of information can be gleaned from each arrangement.

SOUTH

4	9	2
3	5	7
8	1	6

THE PERIOD OF SEVEN

We are currently living through the period of seven, which started in 1984 and will not end until the year 2003. This means that during this period, the number seven is deemed to be very lucky. The Lo Shu square for this period is shown here and, through an interpretation of the numbers, it describes the fortunate and less fortunate sectors up to the year 2003.

SOUTH

6	2	4
5	7	9
1	3	8

The original nine-sector Lo Shu square has the number five in the center. The numbers are arranged so that the sum of any three numbers, taken vertically, horizontally, or diagonally, is 15. In flying star feng shui, the numbers move from grid to grid and they are then interpreted according to which one is in which square. Each of the eight grids on the outside of the square represents a corner of the home. For analysis, the center is the ninth grid. South is placed on top, according to tradition, for presentation purposes only. Use a compass to identify the actual corners of your home.

During the period of seven, the sickness stars, two and five, are located in the south and east respectively. This is interpreted to mean that if the main door of your home is located in either of these sectors, residents will be more susceptible to sickness. It also means that those sleeping in bedrooms located in these sectors are more prone to suffering ill-health.

The analysis will be more accurate when investigation is also conducted on the star numerals during the year and month in question. When all of the star numerals two and five occur together in the same sector, illness is definite during that month and year for people whose bedrooms are in that sector. When you become aware of the time when you are more prone to falling ill, do not sleep in the room afflicted by the numerals two or five for that month.

Year	Star numeral 2 is in the	Star numeral 5 is in the
1997	Southeast	West
1998	Center	Northeast
1999	Northwest	South
2000	West	North
2001	Northeast	Southwest
2002	South	East
2003	North	Southeast
2004	Southwest	Center
2005	East	Northwest
2006	Southeast	West

Year	Month 1	Month 2	Month 3	Month 4	Month 5
1997	Southwest	East Northwest	Southeast West	Northeast	South Northwest
1998	Northeast	Northwest South	West North	Northeast Southwest	South East
1999	Northeast Southwest	South East	North Southeast	Southwest	East Northwest
2000	Southwest	East Northwest	Southeast West	Northeast	Northwest South
2001	Northeast	Northwest South	West North	Northeast Southwest	South East

ROOMS TO AVOID DURING SPECIFIC PERIODS
The yearly reference table
(*based on the lunar year)

The table opposite shows where the star five and star two occur together. The star two combined with star five is very dangerous, and will bring sickness.

THE MONTHLY REFERENCE TABLES.
(*based on the lunar months)

The table below indicates the dangerous sectors during each of the 12 lunar months over the next five years. These are the sectors where the star

Based on the reference table left, rooms in the south are prone to illness in 1999. In 2002 rooms in the south and east should be avoided and in 2005 rooms in the east should be avoided.

numerals two and five are located during that month. In the years 1998 and 2001 there are 13 months, so one of the months has been doubled.

Match where the star numerals two and five fall during the months indicated with those of the annual star numerals and the 20-year period star numerals.

If the twos and fives occur together, that sector will become dangerous and anyone occupying a room in an afflicted sector would do well to leave it for that time. Be particularly careful when the star numerals two and five fall into the east sector. This is because the eastern sector is afflicted with the five in the 20-year period flying star. The danger months and the directions are marked. When there are two dots, it means that both the sectors indicated are dangerous.

Month 6	Month 7	Month 8	Month 9	Month 10	Month 11	Month 12
West North	Northeast Southwest	South East	North Southeast	Southwest	East Northwest	Southeast West
South East	North Southeast	Southwest	East Northwest	Southeast West	Northeast	Northwest South
Southeast West	Northeast	Northwest South	West North	Northeast Southwest	South East	North Southeast
West North	Northeast Southwest	South East	North Southeast	Southwest	East Northwest	Southeast West
North Southeast	Southwest	East Northwest	Southeast West	Northeast	Northwest South	West North

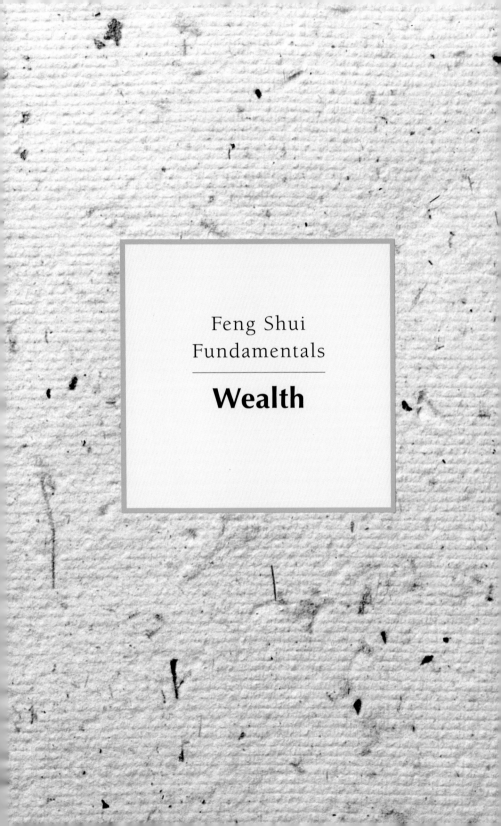

Feng Shui
Fundamentals

Wealth

WEALTH FENG SHUI

THE DIRECTION SOUTH-EAST

財
官
田

The trigram that represents the prosperity aspiration is Sun and, according to the Later Heaven Arrangement, it is placed in the southeast. This is therefore the corner of the home or office that represents wealth, and if this corner has good feng shui, then the wealth aspirations of the household have been effectively energized. If this corner has bad feng shui, however, inauspicious money luck will befall the household, leading to loss and failure in business. To activate wealth feng shui it is therefore vital to ensure that any negative energy is removed or deflected from the southeast corner of your home or office.

THE WOOD ELEMENT

The element of the southeast location is wood, symbolized by plants and all things made of wood, and this is most significant when practicing feng shui, since identifying the relevant and applicable element to activate is vital to the process. It suggests that placing a plant in the southeast, for instance, will be excellent wealth feng shui. Moreover, from the cycles shown here, you will see further attributes of the wood element.

▧ Wood is produced by water, so it will benefit from water.
▧ Wood itself produces fire, so fire will exhaust it.
▧ Wood is destroyed by metal, so metal will harm it.

■ Wood destroys earth, so it will overwhelm earth.

From studying these attributes we learn that to energize the element of the southeast we should use objects that symbolize both the wood and water elements, and avoid those belonging to the metal element. However, it is important to remember that in feng shui balance is everything. Too much of any one element will overwhelm the others. Elements used subtly will reinforce each other.

SUN

This trigram has two solid yang lines above a broken yin line, which signifies the wind that brings prosperity. The image conjured by this trigram is of·the wind scattering seeds to all corners of the earth. The seeds then fall to the ground, penetrate the soil, and begin to germinate. Very soon a plant grows. It blooms and flowers, producing more seeds, which are scattered again by the wind, and the cycle of prosperity is repeated over and over again. Thus is wealth creation symbolized. If you activate this trigram in your home, it is believed that all your financial projects will succeed.

THE CHINESE VIEW OF WEALTH

Becoming rich and prosperous is an almost universal aspiration of the Chinese people. They make no secret of this fact. Material possessions are a primary consideration if you wish to be seen as a success, and the Chinese preoccupation with prosperity is reflected in many of their cultural practices.

The Chinese greeting when they see someone is seldom, "Hello, how are you?" but "Are you well, have you eaten?" This preoccupation with eating has its roots in material welfare. The rice bowl is often symbolic of this well-being, so there are those who regard a golden rice bowl as signifying wealth.

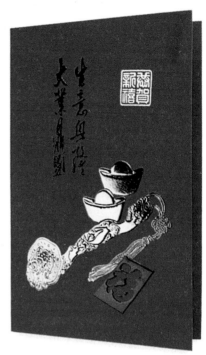

The Chinese send red or gold cards during the New Year festival.

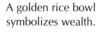

A golden rice bowl symbolizes wealth.

During the lunar New Year celebrations – the most important annual festival – the Chinese send cards that are always printed in red (to signify an auspicious occasion) or gold (to signify wealth) and the greeting is always Kung Hei Fatt Choy, or "congratulations and may you become more prosperous". The Chinese New Year greeting never wavers from these four words!

For the Chinese, wishing friends and loved ones prosperity during the New Year is considered an important part of the celebrations. The Chinese never visit each other's homes empty-handed; they always bring some "gold" along. One favorite present is the gift of mandarin oranges because they signify kum, or gold, once again encouraging wealth in the home.

There are other symbols of prosperity used during the 15 days of the Chinese New Year – either displayed at home as part of the New Year feng shui or sent as gifts to close friends and relatives, including the following:

- ⊠ The pineapple fruit, which indicates that good luck is coming.
- ⊠ A pair of potted lime plants dripping with orange fruits, which signifies wealth luck.
- ⊠ A potted jade plant to wish the recipient great prosperity.

The pineapple is often displayed as a symbol of good luck during the Chinese New Year.

This book focuses exclusively on the wealth-generating aspects of feng shui and this book has proved difficult to write because there are so many symbols, so many different methods, and so many ways of activating wealth feng shui. Just remember that the effectiveness of the methods presented here will work differently for different people, depending on other factors, particularly the balance of the individual's Tien Ti Ren luck.

The pursuit of material wealth represents such a big part of the Chinese psyche that many feng shui guidelines focus on it. The promise of prosperity is probably what has kept the practice of feng shui alive all these centuries. Passed on from father to son, prosperity feng shui continues to be practiced by modern day descendants.

BALANCE

When you practice feng shui, do not worry if you cannot act upon every suggestion. More is not necessarily always better. Balance is vital. Sometimes just energizing one method or activating one auspicious direction may be sufficient. An excellent indicator that your feng shui is working is when you find yourself suddenly becoming very busy. Good feng shui brings opportunity, but for this to crystallize into wealth, you will have to work at making full use of the luck that has come your way.

ENERGIZING THE WOOD ELEMENT

In feng shui, each of the five elements is activated when objects belonging to that particular element group are present. To energize the wood element of the southeast wealth corner, the sector known as "small wood," the best method is to use as many plants as possible, especially small ones. Almost any kind of plant will do, as long as they look healthy and vigorous. For this reason you can even use artificial plants if you like. However, some plants are more auspicious than others, while some are not recommended at all.

GOOD-FORTUNE PLANTS

Feng shui always recommends the use of broad-leaved plants that look healthy and green. If flowering plants or cut flowers are used, they should always look fresh and bright. Sickly or dead-looking plants and flowers emit a negative energy that signifies loss. You should therefore never use dried flowers in this corner. If a plant starts to wilt, throw it out and replace it immediately with healthier-looking plants.

The Chinese jade plant is highly recommended. It has succulent leaves that

Plants should always look healthy and green. If a plant is in poor health, replace it with a healthier specimen.

Avoid plants with thorns, such as these cacti, as they are inauspicious.

COLORS

The wood element is also activated by using green and brown colors – in any shade or hue. Drapes, duvets, carpets, and wallpapers in the southeast should be predominantly greens or browns. You can be as creative as you like when implementing the suggestions here and they are by no means exclusive. Some people use paintings of lush green scenery to activate this corner, others use wooden paneling. Whatever you use, do not overdo it. Balance is vital.

suggest wealth. Affluent Chinese homes display an ornamental plant made from real jade to stimulate prosperity.

The oriental lime plant covered with lots of fruits symbolizes a successful harvest. If this is not available, an orange tree may also be used or an artificial plant. The oranges suggest a tree ripe with gold. It is a most auspicious energizer to display in the home.

INAUSPICIOUS PLANTS

Avoid displaying stunted or deformed plants, such as bonsai or cactus. Although these look quaint and can be exquisitely beautiful, the suggestion of stunted development is not good. Auspicious feng shui always suggests abundant growth.

OTHER OBJECTS

In addition to plants and flowers, other objects made of wood can also be placed in the southeast, but a living plant is always to be preferred. Never have dried or dying plants or driftwood in this corner. Their energy is enervating in a corner that needs plenty of life.

Keep an aquarium with goldfish to attract wealth luck.

USING OBJECTS OF THE WATER ELEMENT

Applying the theory of the productive cycle of the elements indicates that water produces wood, so water features will also activate the southeast to attract wealth luck. Throughout history water has always represented wealth to the Chinese. Many Chinese restaurants use the water element to improve the feng shui of their premises by drawing a fish or water motif around their walls.

This motif can also be drawn on the southeast walls of your living room or, as the Chinese do, you can buy a miniature fountain that keeps the water flowing in a never-ending cycle. This small movement of water is considered most auspicious and, when used in stores and offices, it often represents good luck in increasing turnover. A well-lit aquarium with goldfish is also a good idea. The bubbling oxygenators represent excellent feng shui. If you keep fish, make sure there are nine, of which eight should be red or gold and one black. The black fish will absorb any bad luck that inadvertently enters the corner. It is most auspicious to

keep arrowanas – a tropical fish that is universally acknowledged as the best feng shui fish.

If your room is large or you wish to activate water in the southeast of your garden for wealth luck, you can be very ambitious and install any one of the following water features.

- ▨ A small fish pond filled with good-fortune carp, as long as it is to the left of your front door.
- ▨ A small waterfall, which, if it also happens to face the front door of your home, is considered so auspicious as to bring you enormous wealth luck.

Artificial waterfalls are extremely popular with the Chinese in southeast Asia, and many have had their bank balances expanded after installing such a garden feature. Again take note of balance. Do not have a waterfall that is so large as to overwhelm the house.

A small artificial waterfall in the garden is extremely auspicious.

SYMBOLS OF PROSPERITY

There is a great deal of symbolism in the practice of feng shui. Central to this is the belief that displaying auspicious objects around the home attracts good-luck energies, especially when they are correctly displayed and placed in the right corners of the home. Thus, prosperity symbols should abound, since they represent money in various forms, particularly what passed as money in the past.

Fake gold and silver ingots made in the traditional boat shape are very popular, especially during the lunar New Year when they are freely displayed in the home. The fact that such pretend gold belongs to the metal element does not stop it from being placed near the main entrance, irrespective of the compass location of the front door.

The Chinese display fake gold ingots during their New Year celebrations to bring good luck.

ANCIENT CHINESE COINS

Probably the most popular symbols, however, are old Chinese coins with a square hole in the center. These coins have tremendous potency, especially when they are energized with red thread. There are many ways of using this particular good-fortune symbol.

USING COINS

Hang the coins, tied together with red thread, as mobiles in the southeast corner of the home. Do not overdo this. Three coins are sufficient.

Bury nine of these coins in a pathway just under the pavement that leads to your home, or if you live in an apartment, stick them under a mat just outside your door. This represents money making its way to your doorstep. Make sure red thread has been tied round the coins. If you run a retail store, this will greatly increase your sales and your turnover.

Tape three coins tied with red thread on the southeast corner of your work table or desk to energize money luck!

Place coins under paving stones and let the pathway curve. This is excellent prosperity feng shui.

Another excellent way of using the coins is to tie three coins together with red thread and then stick them onto your sales invoice files, check book, or any folder that has to do with your income. The coins are said to be powerful activators when used this way. Turnover increases and your income will receive healthy doses of unexpected good luck.

Tie three coins with red thread and attach them to your ledger book.

INDIVIDUAL WEALTH ORIENTATIONS

THE COMPASS FORMULA

Also known as the Pa Kua Lo Shu formula (Kua formula for short), this method of investigating personal prosperity orientations was given to the author's feng shui Master by an old Taiwan feng shui Grand Master who was a legend in his time. As the personal consultant of many of Taiwan's richest men of the time, Master Chan Chuan Huay was an expert on wealth feng shui and was particularly well schooled in the science of water feng shui. He was also in possession of this Kua formula and used it with spectacular success for his clients, many of whom founded huge business conglomerates that are managed today by their heirs and descendants. It is no coincidence that the small island of Taiwan is so rich. Feng shui has always been widely practiced there.

THE THREE-LEGGED FROG

The three-legged frog with a coin in its mouth and surrounded by yet more coins signifies an abundance of riches. A frog is already a good-fortune symbol, but the three-legged frog is believed to symbolize something quite special. These frogs are widely used and so are not difficult to purchase in Chinese emporiums.

If your Kua number is:

1	east group
2	west group
3	east group
4	east group
5	west group
6	west group
7	west group
8	west group
9	east group

If you do find one and wish to display it in the home, the best place is on a low table in the living room in full view of the main door. Do not place the frog on the floor. It is always advisable to elevate good-fortune symbols slightly.

THE KUA FORMULA

Number 5 is not used in the Kua formula, although for clarity it is listed below. Females should use 8 instead of 5 and males 2.

Your Wealth orientation is:

SOUTHEAST for both males and females

NORTHEAST for both males and females

SOUTH for both males and females

NORTH for both males and females

NORTHEAST for males and
SOUTHWEST for females

WEST for both males and females

NORTHWEST for both males and females

SOUTHWEST for both males and females

EAST for both males and females

THE KUA FORMULA

Calculate your Kua number as follows. Add the last two digits of your Chinese year of birth. e.g. **1967, 6+7=13**.
If the sum is higher than ten, reduce to a single digit, thus **1+3=4**.

Males	Females
Subtract from	Add
10	**5**
thus	thus
10-4	5+4
=6	=9
So, for men born in	So, for women born in
1967	**1967**
the Kua number is	the Kua number is
6	**9**

Now check against this table for your wealth direction and location.

SLEEPING, DINING, AND COOKING FOR WEALTH

Once you know your wealth direction, you can begin to activate it to enhance your income, by arranging your bed and sitting orientations within the home. It is by activating and using these personalized directions that feng shui becomes most potent.

THE OVEN 'MOUTH'

How your food is cooked also has a bearing on the quality of your luck. For the Chinese, whose staple food is rice, it is easy to orient the rice cooker so that its oven "mouth" is facing the wealth direction. The "mouth" is the place where the electricity enters the cooker, based on the hypotheses that the source of the energy that cooks the rice must come from the wealth direction, because it brings wealth (food) with it.

YOUR BED

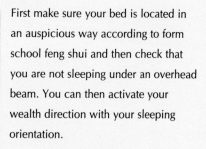

First make sure your bed is located in an auspicious way according to form school feng shui and then check that you are not sleeping under an overhead beam. You can then activate your wealth direction with your sleeping orientation.

The arrow shows you how to take the direction in the correct way. Note that the head must be pointed in the wealth direction. If you and your spouse have different wealth directions, either sleep in two separate beds or let the direction of the breadwinner prevail. Note also that the bed is placed diagonally to the door and the foot of the bed does not point to the door.

For Western homes, the orientation to get right is the source of energy to your oven or cooker This takes a bit of doing, but is worth it since getting the oven "mouth" correctly oriented is an important part of wealth feng shui.

YOUR DINING TABLE

Select the chair that allows you to sit facing your wealth direction. The arrows show you how to take the direction.

It is a good idea to place a full length mirror in the dining room to reflect the food on the table. This doubles the meal and is regarded as excellent wealth feng shui. Make sure the mirror is higher than the tallest person in the home.

THE CHINESE GODS OF WEALTH

Many Chinese homes display gods of wealth. These deities are seldom worshipped in a religious fashion, but displayed in rooms and offices to symbolize the importance of the wealth aspiration. If you wish to do the same, you can find them in a Chinese supermarket in any major Western city.

FUK, LUK, AND SAU

The most popular are the three star gods, collectively referred to as Fuk, Luk, and Sau, which literally translated means wealth, affluence, and longevity. They are present in almost all Chinese homes and are believed to bring great good luck to households, especially wealth luck.

Fuk, Luk, and Sau always stand alongside one another.

- Fuk symbolizes happiness and wealth, stands a head taller, and is placed in the center.
- Luk, the god of high rank and affluence, holds the scepter of power and authority. He stands on the right.
- Sau, with his domed head and carrying a peach in one hand and a walking stick in the other, is often accompanied by a deer and stands on the left.

Wealthy Chinese families in Hong Kong, Taiwan, and Singapore often commission specially crafted giant-sized figurines of **Fuk, Luk, and Sau** to display in special rooms designed to house them. Middle class families buy ceramic, enamel, or wooden replicas and these are believed to be just as symbolically effective.

OTHER PERSONIFICATIONS OF WEALTH

There are a number of other deities who are believed to bring wealth luck into households.

The laughing Buddha.

THE LAUGHING BUDDHA

This is an extremely popular deity with business people. This fat Buddha, with a broadly smiling face and a huge fat belly, can often be seen, usually in standing form, in restaurants and jewelry stores. The laughing Buddha is also portrayed fanning himself while seated on a bag of gold (depicting wealth), or surrounded by a group of five children.

TSAI SHEN YEH

Popular with the Cantonese, this is another prosperity god. He has a fierce countenance and he is seated on a tiger. If you place him directly facing the main door, wealth will be attracted into the home.

KUAN KUNG

Also known as Kuan Ti, Kuan Kung is a popular deity. He is said to bring both prosperity and protection, and is also the powerful god of war. The story of Kuan Kung is documented in the Romance of the Three Kingdoms. Displaying his fierce countenance in the living room, preferably facing the main door, is sufficient to attract good fortune.

Kuan Kung.

WONG CHOY SAN

Another popular wealth deity, he is widely believed to be extremely generous to households that display him. He is often depicted carrying a rat, with gold bars placed at his feet.

Wong Choy San.

~89~

FENG SHUI FOR BUSINESS AND COMMERCE

THE RETAIL STORE

If you own a retail store, energizing wealth luck through feng shui depends on what sort of business you are in. Determine the element that best repre-sents the things you sell, and then acti-vate the relevant compass direction corner that symbolizes that element. Display objects and paintings, or decorate with motifs suggestive of the element. Some categories of businesses and their matching elements are shown here.

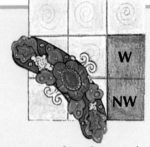

Activate **metal** (northwest and west) if you are in the jewelry or boutique business. Avoid using red, and place a windchime in the metal corners. Placing a crystal in the west is also auspicious.

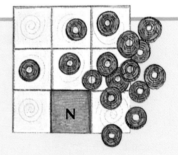

Activate **water** (north) if you are in any business that deals with money. Bank and insurance branches, bars, and even restaurants qualify as water enterprises. Place a water feature in the north and decorate your store with a water motif.

Activate **wood** (the east or southeast) if you run a grocery business or are engaged in selling things made of paper or wood. Place a plant in the east corner of your store.

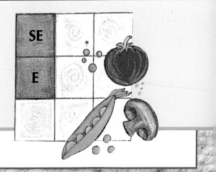

DECORATING IDEAS

Horseshoe-shaped magnets can be used to activate metal. Natural quartz or cut crystals are also very lucky.

One of the best ways of energizing the earth element for business is to display the globe – to develop export markets, twirl it daily

The best and most beautiful way to energize wood is to make the fullest use of plants. Even artificial silk plants are acceptable. However, do not use dried plants or driftwood.

Use lights to activate fire or regularly light a candle in the south. Alternatively, decorate with the fire or sun motif. Effectively activating the fire element will give your store a great reputation.

The water element can be energized by using water motifs or by installing a water feature, such as a small fountain or even a bowl of water. Remember that activating water is good for most businesses.

Activate **fire** (the south) if you are in the catering or restaurant business (cooking connotes fire), or if you are selling light fixtures. Install a bright light, kept on continuously, in the south and at the entrance. A jade plant or small aquarium at the entrance is also auspicious for the business.

Activate **earth** (southwest, northeast and center) if you are in real estate or if you are an architect or developer. Use earth colors for your decor and place natural quartz or faceted lead crystals in the earth sectors of your store or office.

DOUBLING YOUR TURNOVER –
TWO EXCELLENT TIPS

Protecting the cash register is vital. The cash register or credit card machine is the most important item in your store. It symbolizes your revenue and income. First, make sure nothing sharp or pointed is aimed at it: this can be the sharp edge of a protruding corner, an overhead beam, open book shelves, or even a pointed object, such as a pair of scissors or a blade left idly by.

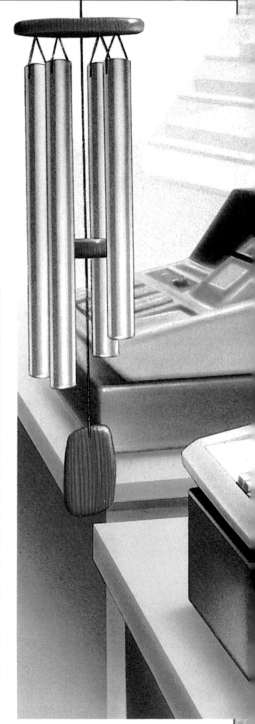

TIP ONE

Hang a windchime immediately above the cash register. Make sure the rods of the chime are hollow, as this is the feature that will encourage the chi to rise. The tinkling sounds of the chimes also encourage the creation of abundant good-fortune chi. There can be any number of the rods on the windchime, except five. If you cannot find a windchime, hang three Chinese coins tied with red thread.

A variation of this popular method is to hang tiny bells at the door. This not only announces a customer's entry, it also attracts good-fortune chi into the store.

Cover the wall next to the cash register with mirror glass. This has the effect of doubling the turnover for your store. You must be able to see the cash register reflected in the mirror, but at the same time, make sure that the mirror does not directly reflect the entrance. Place the mirror on a side wall. Also, make certain that the cash register is not easily visible from outside the store.

Feng Shui
Fundamentals

Love

ROMANCE FENG SHUI

THE DIRECTION SOUTH-WEST

The trigram that represents love and relationships is the yin trigram Kun and, according to the Later Heaven Arrangement of trigrams, this is placed in the southwest. This is the corner of any home or room that represents romance, love, and marriage. If this corner has good feng shui, the marriage and love aspirations of the members of the household will be positively energized.

If this corner has bad feng shui, however, bad marriage luck will befall the household, leading to divorce, loneliness, unhappiness, and an almost total absence of marriage opportunities for the sons and daughters of the family. Thus romance feng shui should always start with an examination of this sector of the room or home.

THE EARTH ELEMENT

The element of the southwest corner is earth, symbolized by crystals, stones, boulders, and all things from the ground. Identifying the relevant element to activate is a vital part of the application. It suggests that placing, for instance, a boulder in the southwest corner of the garden will activate excellent romance and marriage opportunities for all the unattached residents of the house.

- ⊞ Earth is produced by fire, so fire is said to be good for it.
- ⊞ Earth itself produces metal, so metal is said to exhaust it.
- ⊞ Earth is destroyed by wood, so wood is said to be harmful to it.
- ⊞ Earth destroys water, so it is said to overcome water.

From these attributes we know that to strengthen the element of the southwest we can use objects that symbolize both the earth and the fire elements, but we should avoid the wood element.

The Later Heaven Arrangement of trigrams is used inside the home.

KUN

 This trigram is made up of three broken yin lines. Kun is the trigram that symbolizes mother earth. Inherent to this trigram is the concept of the ideal matriarch, all that is receptive and ultimate yin energy. Kun symbolizes the person who accepts all the responsibilities of the family, performing the crucial role of keeping the family together, giving birth, raising children, and dispensing love and kindness, in spite of hard work. Like the earth, the matriarch grows everything and receives everything back. The earth supports mountains, cradles the oceans, and is always enduring. This is a powerful trigram.

One of the best representations of it is a mountain, and a painting of mountains hung in the Kun corner brings extraordinary romantic luck.

ENERGIZING THE EARTH ELEMENT

In feng shui, each of the five elements is activated when objects belonging to it are present. One of the best objects to use to energize the earth element of the southwest romance corner is a crystal, especially natural quartz crystal dug up from the earth.

CRYSTALS

Raw amethyst, quartz, or other natural crystals will be extremely harmonious with the southwest sector. In addition, other minerals and metals from the earth are effective, although the energies created by the display of crystals is particularly positive. If you like, you can also use artificial, manmade lead crystals, which may be paperweights or even good-fortune symbols fashioned out of crystal and displayed on your table top.

The facets of crystal and cut glass are especially potent when combined with light.

Crystal chandeliers are said to attract tremendous good luck. Hung in the southwest corner of a room, a chandelier brings wonderful romantic and relationship luck. Chandeliers made with faceted crystal balls are also suitable in other corners of a room.

When hung in the center of the house, they shower the home with extremely auspicious family luck. This is because the center of any home, the heart of the residence, is also signified by the earth element and should represent the area of maximum energy or chi concentration. For this reason, feng shui also warns against locating kitchens, store rooms, and toilets in the center of a home, because all of these destroy beneficial chi.

Natural quartz crystal and artificial crystal paperweights.

~98~

Crystal chandeliers, if you can afford them, make excellent feng shui energizers. The combination of crystal (earth element) and light (fire element) usually spells success and happiness.

If you cannot afford a chandelier, buy a few loose crystal balls and hang them near a light or on windows that are bathed with sunshine. This brings valuable yang energies into the home, sometimes causing the sunlight to break up into colorful rainbows.

OTHER GOOD-FORTUNE EARTH OBJECTS

Large, round decorative earthenware jars and pots are excellent for the southwest corners of rooms. Place peacock feathers, artificial silk flowers, or, better still, freshly cut flowers inside these jars. On no account display dried or dead flowers or plants, not even decorative driftwood. Dead wood and dried plants signify the death of a romantic relationship.

A globe is wonderfully symbolic of mother earth. This object has been found to be very effective for stimulating the southwest corners of rooms. Place it on a table top and activate it daily by spinning it round. This creates wonderful yang energy that balances the yin of the southwest corner exceedingly well.

Any decorated pot or stone jar will activate the earth element in the romance corner.

COLORS

The earth element is also activated by using earth tones and hues and so curtains, duvets, carpets, and wallpaper in the southwest should contain predominantly earth colors. You can be as creative as you like when implementing the suggestions here, and they are by no means exclusive. Some people use paintings of mountain scenery to activate this corner. Whatever you use, however, do not overdo it. Stay balanced. In feng shui, less is often better than more.

A SPECIAL TIP

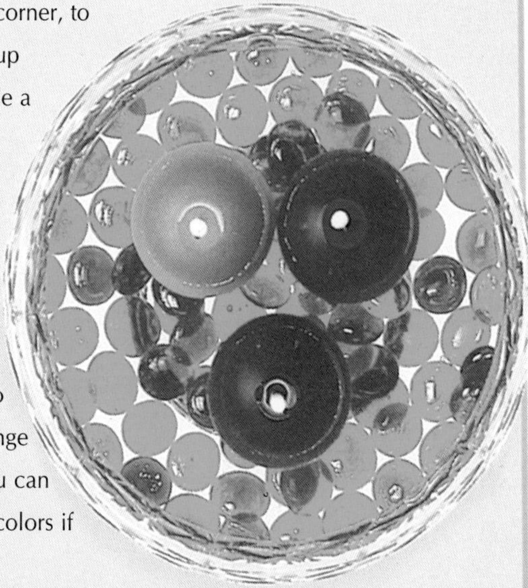

A tip for energizing the southwest corner, to
attract suitable partners for grown-up
daughters, is to place pebbles inside a
shallow glass or crystal bowl, fill it
with water, float some flowers on
top, if you have any and place a
floating candle in the center. This
brings together a basket of
elements and lighting the candle
each day will attract vital energy to
the corner. If you use flowers, change
both them and the water daily. You can
use pebbles of any color. Mix the colors if
you wish.

Earth colored
soft furnishings are
used to activate the
earth element.

USING OBJECTS OF THE FIRE ELEMENT

Applying the theory of the productive cycle of the elements, we also note that fire produces earth, so fire element features can also activate the southwest to energize marriage and relationship luck. For the Chinese, the color red, which is of the fire element, represents happiness, festivity, and celebrations. This is evident at Chinese weddings, where the bride always wears red.

The bride is wearing red, the color that symbolizes happiness and celebration.

The southwest sector of any room can also be favorably stimulated by locating the fireplace in this corner. This will be a powerful activator, particularly during the cold winter months when the fire burns and brings welcome warmth and good cheer into the home.

EARTH AND FIRE

Both earth and fire motifs can be painted or stenciled onto the southwest walls of your living room or incorporated into wall designs or soft furnishings.

Lights are another potent feng shui tool that can be used to manipulate the balance of elements. Always make sure that there is a bright light in the southwest corner. Keeping the corner well lit prevents the energies there from getting stale, and the favorable chi thus created will never become stagnant.

The element of the southwest corner, which represents love is earth, and earth motifs are placed to activate romantic relationships.

The sun motif is a powerful symbol of the fire element and, when placed in the southwest, it complements the earth element admirably.

The love knot worked in red is extremely effective when used for the southwest corner. It was a great favorite with Chinese ladies of an earlier era. The knot does not have an end and it appears to go on forever and is a symbol of undying love.

INDIVIDUAL MARRIAGE ORIENTATIONS

THE COMPASS FORMULA

According to the feng shui Masters, the family direction can be activated to attract excellent relationship luck within the family, not just between husband and wife, but also between parents and children. Couples having problems conceiving children can also use this formula to orient their sleeping directions, thereby correcting the problem. Most of all, however, the formula is especially useful for ensuring that husbands and wives stay happily together.

THE CHINESE VIEW OF LOVE AND ROMANCE

The Chinese view lasting relationships as the ultimate in double happiness. Satisfaction in love and love-making is considered a principal ingredient of a worthy and successful life. To the Chinese, a happy love life adds to health and longevity, and feng shui directly addresses this dimension of living by offering various suggestions for improving our chances of attaining this happiness.

Feng shui can be used to enhance relationship prospects and bring about happiness and mutual respect. It does not promise fidelity within the marriage or

If your Kua number is:

1 east group

2 west group

3 east group

4 east group

5 west group

6 west group

7 west group

8 west group

9 east group

relationship, but it can enhance and strengthen the family unit and, by so doing, offer harmony and peace to everyone within the home.

THE KUA FORMULA

Number 5 is not used in the Kua formula, although for clarity it is listed below. Females should use 8 instead of 5 and males 2.

Your Marriage/Family orientation is:

SOUTH for both males and females

NORTHWEST for both males and females

SOUTHEAST for both males and females

EAST for both males and females

NORTHWEST for males and **WEST** for females

SOUTHWEST for both males and females

NORTHEAST for both males and females

WEST for both males and females

NORTH for both males and females

THE KUA FORMULA

Add the last two digits of your Chinese year of birth. e.g. **1978**, 7+8=15
If the sum is higher than ten, always reduce to a single digit, thus **1+5=6**

Males	Females
Subtract from	Add
10	**5**
thus	thus
10-6	**5+6**
=4	**=11**
So, for men born in	**1+1=2**
	So, for women born in
1978	**1978**
the Kua number is	the Kua number is
4	**7**

Now check against this table for your marriage and family direction.

INSIDE THE BEDROOM

While it is ideal to have a regular-shaped bedroom located in the part of the home that corresponds to your marriage and family direction, this is not always possible. You should try very hard to have your head pointed in your personal direction. If you cannot do this make sure you do not have it pointed toward any of your four inauspicious directions. Select one of the other three that is suitable for you.

harmonious relationship with your loved one, you are strongly advised to cover up mirrors installed on closet doors and to move your dressing table – with its inevitable mirror – into another room.

TABOOS TO BE OBSERVED AND AVOIDED

Never sleep with a mirror facing your bed. A television is regarded as being the same as a mirror, as it also reflects your image. If you do have a television in the bedroom, make sure you cover it when it is not in use. A mirror in the bedroom is one of the most harmful feng shui features. Mirrors facing the bed, in reflecting the couple, suggest interference from outside and consequently a marriage or relationship may fall apart through infidelity. If you want to have a

Never sleep under an exposed, overhead beam. The severity of the adverse effect depends on where the beam crosses the bed. If it cuts the bed in half, in addition to causing severe headaches, it also symbolically separates the couple sleeping underneath. If the beam is pressing on the heads of the couple, it will cause petty disagreements that develop into severe quarrels. If it is by the side of the bed, the effect is lessened. If your bed is affected by a beam, move the bed out of the way. If this is not possible, try to camouflage it in some way.

Never sleep on a bed placed directly in front of the door to the bedroom, irrespective of your sleeping direction. It does not matter whether your head or your feet point toward the door, this bed position is equally harmful. One or both members of the couple will suffer from ill health. There will be no time for love and health becomes a problem. Move the bed out of the way of the door or place some kind of divider in the way.

Never sleep with the sharp edge of a protruding corner pointed at you. This is a common problem. Many bedrooms have such corners and they are as harmful as pillars. The sharp edge of the corner is one of the most deadly forms of poison arrows that bring shar chi, or killing breath. The solution to this problem is to block off or camouflage the corner. Using plants is an ideal solution in the living room, but the presence of plants is not such a good idea in the bedroom. It is better to use a piece of furniture to conceal the sharp edge.

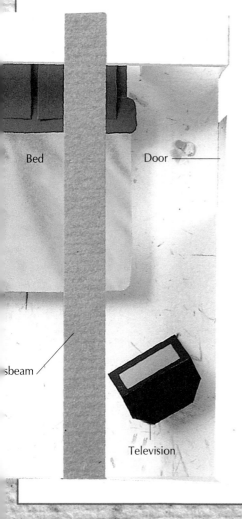

Bed

Door

sbeam

Television

This bedroom has a disastrous feng shui arrangement. The bed is being attacked by poison arrows, there is a television acting as a mirror, a crossbeam is pressing on the bed, and ill health is being invited in through the door.

ENHANCING YOUR MARRIAGE PROSPECTS

ACTIVATING YOUR MARRIAGE AND LOVE CORNER

婚姻

For those keen on adding sparkle and new energy to their love lives and enhancing their marriage prospects, Kua formula feng shui offers some simple, yet effective, suggestions. While much of bedroom feng shui focuses on harnessing good fortune for those already married, combining the Kua formula with the use of good-fortune symbols can sometimes work wonders in bringing about a more active and enjoyable social and love life for single people.

HOW TO DO IT

▓ Check your personal marriage and family direction based on your Kua number (see pages 104–105).

▓ Select a room in your home that you wish to activate. It should be a room where you spend a great deal of time, but preferably not your bedroom. The living room or the study or work room is usually ideal.

▓ Stand in the center of the room and take your compass bearings. Identify the corner of the room that represents your marriage and family direction. Do this by superimposing an imaginary grid of nine sectors, then accurately mark out the sector that represents your marriage corner. This is the area of the room you will need to activate.

▓ Next, select from the good fortune symbols listed opposite. You can buy these items or make your own symbols.

~108~

If you have difficulty finding ducks, lovebirds are also excellent symbols of love. You can even keep live budgerigars in your love corner, but you should always keep them in a pair.

Ducks should be displayed as a pair – never singly, nor too many of them. One pair of ducks signifies a young couple in love. These ducks may be activated by hanging a painting of them or ornamental ducks made of wood or lacquer may be used.

The Chinese love the peony, or mou tan flower, a cherished symbol of love. Most Chinese homes have at least one painting of this species of flower, especially homes where there are grown-up daughters.

SYMBOLS OF ROMANCE AND LOVE

The Chinese have several symbols that signify romance and conjugal happiness. Apart from the powerful double happiness symbol, which can be reproduced and hung on the wall, another wonderful object to display in your love corner is a pair of mandarin ducks.

Western symbols can also be used for romance luck – hearts, pictures of a bride and groom, wedding bouquets, and even paintings of lovers.

CHECKING COMPATIBILITY

EAST AND WEST GROUP PEOPLE

The Kua formula used in compass feng shui also offers one of the most accurate ways of investigating the degree of compatibility between two people. As a general rule, it is highly recommended that people should marry someone from the same group. When an east group person marries a west group person, the compatibility is seriously reduced and, depending on the individual Kua numbers of both, the incompatibility can be quite severe, sometimes so serious that both parties eventually end up harming each other. Perhaps the most famous case of this kind of incompatibility was the marriage between Britain's HRH Prince Charles and Princess Diana, which ended in separation and misery.

EXAMPLE

If your Kua number is three, then the best match for you will be someone with the Kua number one, your sheng chi. He or she will not only make you happy, but will also bring you luck. At the same time people with Kua numbers nine, three, and four are also compatible. Those with Kua number three, therefore, should be wary about becoming involved with people whose Kua numbers are other than those indicated.

COMPATIBLE KUA NUMBERS

Your Kua No.	Sheng Chi Kua	Tien Yi Kua	Nien Yen Kua	Fu Wei Kua
1	3	4	1	9
2	7	8 (m) 8&5 (f)	2&5 (m) 2 (f)	6
3	1	9	3	4
4	9	1	4	3
5	7 (m) 6 (f)	8 (m) 2 (f)	5	6 (m) 7 (f)
6	8 (m) 8&5 (f)	7	6	2&5 (m) 2 (f)
7	2&5 (m) 2 (f)	6	7	8 (m) 8&5 (f)
8	6	2&5 (m) 2 (f)	8 (m) 8&5 (f)	7
9	4	3	9	1

The table above indicates the degrees of compatibility between people of different Kua numbers. Use it to check the compatibility between you and your loved one. Remember that the key to unlocking the meanings lies in your Kua number which you can work out from the formula given on page 105. Males with Kua number five should follow the numbers with (m) after and females with Kua number five should use the numbers with (f) after. The table refers to Kua numbers that are compatible to your Kua number. Note that east group people are always compatible with others of the east group and west group people with others of the west. The degree of compatibility is described as follows.

※ Sheng Chi Kua: extremely compatible; your partner will bring you excellent luck.

※ Tien Yi Kua: very compatible, your partner looks after your health well.

※ Nien Yen Kua: extremely compatible; a most harmonious and happy relationship.

※ Fu Wei Kua: very compatible; your partner is supportive and encouraging.

INCOMPATIBLE KUA NUMBERS

Your Kua No.	Ho Hai Kua	Wu Kwei Kua	Lui Sha Kua	Chueh Ming Kua
1	6	2&5 (m)	7	8&5 (i)
2	9	1	3	4
3	8&5 (m)	7	2&5 (m)	6
4	7	8&5 (i)	6	2&5 (m)
5	9 (m) 3 (i)	1 (m) 4 (i)	3 (m) 9 (i)	4 (m) 1 (i)
6	1	9	4	3
7	4	3	1	9
8	3	4	9	1
9	2&5 (m)	6	8&5 (i)	7

Males with Kua number five should follow the numbers with (m) after and females with Kua number five should follow the numbers with (f) after. The numbers in the table refer to Kua numbers that are incompatible with your Kua number. Note that east group people are incompatible with west group people and vice versa. These numbers refer only to Kua numbers and not anything else. The degree of incompatibility is described as follows.

※ Ho Hai Kua: your partner will cause you accidents and mishaps. The relationship is not smooth.

※ Wu Kwei Kua: very incompatible; both of you will quarrel constantly and there is anger in the relationship. This is the five ghosts relationship, suggesting that outside parties will succeed in causing problems between the two of you.

EXAMPLE

If your Kua number is eight, then
your most dangerous match is
someone with the Kua number
one, which represents total loss for
you, but Kua numbers nine, four,
and three are also incompatible
and best avoided. There can be no
happiness in a long-term
relationship with people who
have these Kua numbers.

※ Lui Sha Kua: extremely incompatible;
your partner will cause you grievous
harm and immense heartbreak. This is
the six killings description, it is far
better to part.

※ Chueh Ming Kua: totally and
irretrievably incompatible.
Your partner will be the death of you,
figuratively and metaphorically. He
or she could ruin your name, cause
you to lose wealth and break your
heart totally. Avoid this partnerhsip
at all costs.

OTHER SYSTEMS

The east and west group formula
to determine compatibility between
partners complements the astrological
method, which uses the Chinese
ghanzhi system of heavenly stems
and earthly branches, best known
under the Chinese zodiac animal
signs. In the old days, both these
methods, as well as detailed
astrological charts, were drawn up to
investigate compatibility. On
occasion, although the Kua formula
and the ghanzhi system indicate
compatibility, sometimes the
elements (wood, fire, water, metal,
and earth) of the birth charts seriously
override the readings, causing
problems between seemingly
compatible couples. Similarly, the
elements of the birth chart can also
override seeming incompatibility, but
again these
are rare occurrences.

**The five
elements:**
fire, earth, metal,
water, wood.

SPECIFIC FENG SHUI ADVICE FOR WOMEN

A TIP FOR THE MARRIED WOMAN

女性

It is important for women who practice feng shui to remember that this is an ancient science from China. In the past, feng shui was used to create wealth, success, happiness, and prominence for families, particularly the head of the family. Success for a man was often measured not just by his wealth and position, but also by the number of concubines and secondary wives that he had. Indeed, men of stature always had an entire harem of wives. Thus, when you introduce feng shui inspired changes to your house, particularly methods that involve the use of water (which signifies wealth), it is prudent to be very careful.

One of the most important tips passed onto me by a very knowledgeable feng shui Master skilled in the practice of water feng shui was that pools of water in the vicinity of homes should never be located on the right-hand side of the main front door. Whether the pool of water is inside or outside the house, it should always be placed on the left-hand

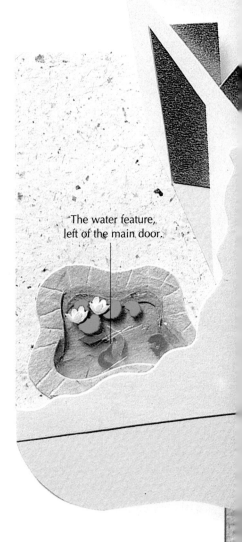

The water feature, left of the main door.

side of the front door. Otherwise, although your husband may be successful and indeed grow wealthy and prosperous, he will also develop a roving eye. At best, if your marriage feng shui has been correctly implemented, he will only look. At worst, however, he could well become unfaithful or leave you altogether.

Therefore, women should ensure that this particular guideline concerning water is scrupulously followed if they want to keep their husbands or partners faithful. The way to determine the location is to stand inside the house looking out. The pool or pond should then be placed on your left side.

Families lucky enough to have swimming pools in their gardens should be especially attentive to this guideline, since the same principle applies to a swimming pool as to any other pool of water. Is it any coincidence that so many successful men all over the world discard their wives after reaching the top?

If you already have a pond or a pool and it is located on the wrong side of your main door, my advice to the lady of the household is to move it, fill it in, or do away with it altogether!

The water feature, left of the main, and sliding doors.

The illustration shows two ponds, one inside the house and one outside. Both ponds are on the left-hand side of the doors – the main door, as well as the sliding doors by the side. Notice that the orientation is taken from inside the house.

Feng Shui
Fundamentals

Fame

FAME FENG SHUI

THE DIRECTION SOUTH

The trigram that represents fame, recognition, and reputation is Li and, according to the Later Heaven Arrangement, this is placed in the south. Thus the southern corner of any home or room represents recognition, reputation, and fame.

THE FIRE ELEMENT

The ruling element of the south is fire, symbolized by bright lights, the sun, the color red, and anything else that suggests fire. Identifying the relevant element to activate is a vital part of feng shui application. It suggests that placing, for instance, a fireplace in the south will activate excellent opportunities for becoming famous and widely respected. This particular type of luck is especially vital for politicians, models, singers, actors, and everyone engaged in professions that require them to be well known and easily recognized.

▨ Fire is produced by wood, so wood is said to be good for it.

- Fire itself produces earth, so earth is said to exhaust it.
- Fire is destroyed by water, so water is said to be harmful to it.
- Fire destroys metal, so it is said to overcome metal.

From these attributes we know that to strengthen the element of the south we can use objects that symbolize both the fire and the wood elements, but that we should strenuously avoid anything belonging to the water element.

LI

 This trigram is made up of one broken, yin line embraced by two unbroken, yang lines. It appears strong on the outside, yet is yielding and weak on the inside.

Li is the trigram that symbolizes the brightness of fire and the dazzle of the sun. It stands for glory and the applause of the masses. It also suggests activity and heat. The symbolism of this trigram is that of a great man who perpetuates the light by rising to prominence. His name and fame illuminate the four corners of the universe, dazzling one and all with his exemplary behavior and his magnificent talents and achievements.

At its ultimate, Li also represents lightning from which we can gauge the intrinsic brilliance of what it stands for. The color of Li is red, the bright and auspicious color that suggests celebrations and happy occasions. Li is the summer, and its energies are more yang than yin.

ENERGIZING THE FIRE ELEMENT

In feng shui, each of the five elements is activated when objects that belong to the element group are present. To energize the fire element of the south, the fame corner, one of the best and easiest methods is to use bright lights – spotlights, crystal chandeliers, twinkling lights. Lights also signify valuable yang energy and so they are especially potent. Indeed, even if fame luck is not necessarily what you particularly want to achieve, installing a bright light and keeping it turned on for at least three hours each evening is always good feng shui.

Lights can be installed in many different ways. Hung from the ceiling, installed as wall brackets, placed on table tops as lamps, or concealed at floor level and shining upward – all these methods are acceptable. In fact, every kind of lighting is acceptable. You can let your own ideas and creativity flow. The lights can be very bright or subdued. The only taboos are that they should be white, yellow, or red, not blue or any of the other yin colors, and that you should refrain from using lampshades or table lamps shaped in a way that creates hostile vibes because they have sharp points or resemble a threatening object. Many modern table lamps have shapes that send out negative energies that are strengthened because of the light itself.

Spotlights can be very effective when shining directly at the south wall of a room. Just be careful that residents do not suffer from the glare. This will represent an excess of yang energy, which is not advisable.

LIGHTING

This table lamp is an excellent feng shui energizer. Its round shape and colors are auspicious.

CRYSTAL CHANDELIERS

If you can afford them, crystal chande-liers make excellent feng shui energizers. The facets of the crystal greatly enhance the light and, if kept switched on, crystal chandeliers in the south corner of any room really do bring auspicious luck to residents.

CRYSTALS

If you cannot afford a chandelier, look for small, faceted crystal balls and hang them with a red thread near a light or in front of windows bathed with sunshine. This brings valuable yang energies into the home, sometimes causing the sunlight to break up into colorful rainbows that are reflected on walls and ceilings.

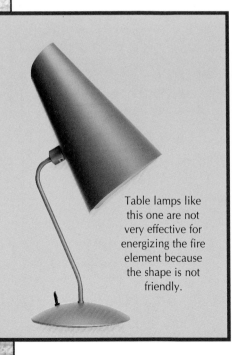

Table lamps like this one are not very effective for energizing the fire element because the shape is not friendly.

THE COLOR RED

The color red is particularly meaningful for activating the recognition factor to maximize success. It is the universally accepted color of good fortune and always present during important festivals and celebrations. Chinese brides almost always wear red, and the birth of a son is celebrated with eggs dyed red. The lunar new year is celebrated by wearing red and the gift of red packets of lucky money to children and employees.

It follows that in feng shui, the color red is also very significant, especially when energizing the south corner of the home to encourage good fortune chi to be created there. It is, therefore, most important to incorporate this most auspicious color in furnishings and decorations if residents wish to benefit from good reputation luck.

Eggs dyed red are used by the Chinese to celebrate the birth of a son.

Red packets are presented to children and employees to celebrate New Year.

Many everyday objects with red as their dominant color can be displayed in the south. These include soft furnishings, such as upholstery, lampshades, drapes, bed spreads, rugs, and carpets.

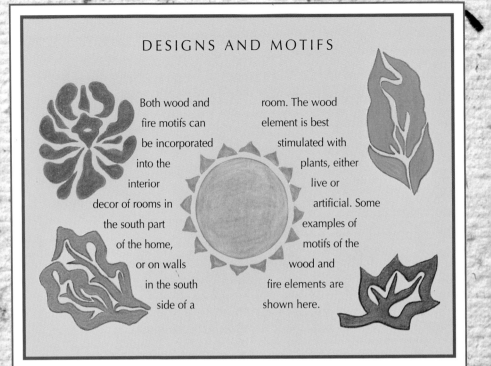

DESIGNS AND MOTIFS

Both wood and fire motifs can be incorporated into the interior decor of rooms in the south part of the home, or on walls in the south side of a room. The wood element is best stimulated with plants, either live or artificial. Some examples of motifs of the wood and fire elements are shown here.

USING OBJECTS OF THE FIRE ELEMENT

The fireplace is, perhaps, one of the most effective ways of energizing the fire element of the south. This is especially significant during winter months when a great deal of yin energy is present, reflected in the cold weather and the long nights. It is during this season that the bright, warm, lively, and cheering yang energy of the fireplace is most needed.

Placing a painting with red as the dominant color or a photograph frame made of wood (since wood produces fire) above the fireplace would be excellent supplements to the fire element.

The warmth of this fire on the south wall restores weak yang energy perfectly.

INDIVIDUAL FAME AND SUCCESS ORIENTATIONS

THE CHINESE VIEW OF REPUTATION

For the Chinese, having a good name and reputation is one of the most important virtues. When you have a reputation for being honorable, honest, worthy, loyal, and possessing great integrity, then you are said to be a superior man. The list of positive attributes can be rather long and many Chinese classics that encompass all three of the major philosophies of China – Taoism, Confucianism, and Buddhism – go to great lengths to advocate and explain the need for living such a life. Individual good name and the good name of the family are most important. Without these, everything else becomes hollow and insubstantial.

Nowhere are the attributes of the superior man more eloquently described than in the I Ching, the Book of Changes, perhaps the greatest classic of Chinese thought to have survived the centuries. Both Taoism and Confucianism derive much of their philosophy from this great text. Feng shui also draws from its teachings and, indeed,

much feng shui interpretation is guided by the meanings attributed to trigrams, the three-lined symbols that feature so prominently in feng shui analysis. These trigrams are the root symbols of the

If your Kua number is:

1 east group

2 west group

3 east group

4 east group

5 west group

6 west group

7 west group

8 west group

9 east group

I Ching's 64 hexagram symbols.

There are many references to the superior man in the I Ching and the underlying assumption of the aspect of feng shui covered in this book is the need to arrange our immediate environment in such a way that we live our lives according to the attributes of a superior man and, more significantly, that we are also recognized, respected, and looked up to as such.

Your Fame and Success orientation is:

SOUTHEAST for both males and females

NORTHEAST for both males and females

SOUTH for both males and females

NORTH for both males and females

NORTHEAST for males and **SOUTHWEST** for females

WEST for both males and females

NORTHWEST for both males and females

SOUTHWEST for both males and females

EAST for both males and females

THE KUA FORMULA

Calculate your Kua number as follows. Add the last two digits of your Chinese year of birth. e.g. **1965**, **6+5=11**.
If the sum is higher than ten, reduce to a single digit, thus **1+1=2**.

Males	Females
Subtract from	Add
10	**5**
thus	thus
10-2	**5+2**
=8	**=7**
So, for men born in	So, for women born in
1965	**1965**
the Kua number is	the Kua number is
8	**7**

Remember that number 5 is not used in the Kua formula though for clarity it is given on the left.
Females should use 8, males 2.

AVOIDING YOUR
TOTAL LOSS DIRECTION

When addressing the important matter of reputation, feng shui particularly warns against having a main door that faces one of your inauspicious directions, especially your chueh ming or total loss direction.

As the name implies, the total loss direction can be dangerous. People whose main door faces their chueh ming usually have more than their fair share of bad luck. None of their ventures seems to succeed, and opportunities slip by with annoying frequency. It is as if something blocks their luck. When their astrological period is bad, having such a main door orientation could even lead to scandal, as well as a major loss of reputation.

Determining your chueh ming direction depends on your Kua number. To safeguard yourself and your good name, you would be advised to check the table here and take counter-measures accordingly. The best way to correct this is to use another door as the main door. If this is not possible, re-orient your main door so that it faces at least one of your auspicious directions.

Your Kua number	Chueh Ming (Males)	Chueh Ming (Females)
1	SOUTH-WEST	SOUTH-WEST
2	NORTH	NORTH
3	WEST	WEST
4	NORTH-EAST	NORTH-EAST
5	NORTH	SOUTH-EAST
6	SOUTH	SOUTH
7	EAST	EAST
8	SOUTH-EAST	SOUTH-EAST
9	NORTH-WEST	NORTH-WEST

HOW TO RE-ORIENTATE YOUR MAIN DOOR

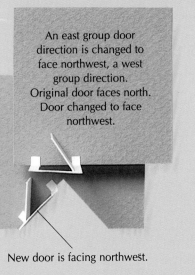

An east group door direction is changed to face northwest, a west group direction.
Original door faces north. Door changed to face northwest.

New door is facing northwest.

Original door faces north.

The same east group door direction (facing north) is now changed to face northeast, a west group direction.

This house has another door that faces west. If north is your chueh ming direction, it would be better to use this second door as your main one.

If your chueh ming direction is north, use the west facing door.

TIPS ABOUT MAIN DOORS

- A solid door is preferable to a glass door.
- A door should open inward and not outward.
- A conventional door is better than a sliding door.
- Let nothing block the outside or inside of the door.
- The door should be neither too big nor too small.
- Do not have two or three doors in a row.

ACTIVATING THE PHOENIX

The feng huang or phoenix holds a very special place in Chinese traditional beliefs. In feng shui it represents the south and is one of the four celestial animals that symbolize classical landscape feng shui. When the crimson phoenix lies in front of the home, in view of the front door, it holds the promise of many wonderful opportunities for residents. Landscape and form school feng shui Masters interpret this to mean the presence of a small boulder or little hillock in front of the home to represent a comfortable footstool. Underlying this supportive role are all the other attributes of the phoenix. Because it presides over the south quadrant of the compass, the phoenix also symbolizes the sun and the warmth of summer – and a rich harvest.

This beautiful creature is believed to be the product of the fire as well as the sun, hence the famous saying – from the ashes, the phoenix rises. This is because fire produces earth (or ashes) in the cycle of the five elements. The phoenix is regarded as very yang, and is said to be wonderful for bringing outstanding fame luck, not only to the breadwinner, but also to the descendants of the household.

Hang a painting of the phoenix on the south wall, above the fireplace, against a red background. This creates auspicious fame luck. You should hang this picture in the living or family room rather than the bedroom or dining room.

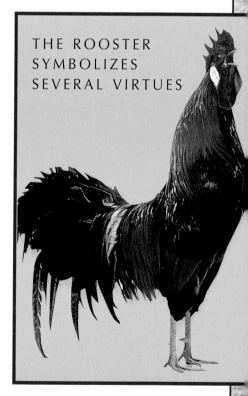

THE ROOSTER
SYMBOLIZES
SEVERAL VIRTUES

- The crown on his head is a mark of his literary skill and his passion for learning.
- The spurs on his feet represent his brave and courageous spirit.
- The rooster is an effective substitute for the phoenix because it is also regarded as the chief embodiment of the yang element, which represents the warmth and life of the universe.
- He crows without fail each morning to announce the dawn of a new day. He is thus faithful and reliable.

In Chinese art, the phoenix is adorned with stunningly beautiful plumage, as befits the king of feathered creatures. However, the phoenix is a legendary creature, and is said to appear only in times of peace and prosperity.

SUBSTITUTES

If you cannot find a painting of a phoenix, any earthenware with the phoenix painted on it can be a good substitute. If you really cannot find a phoenix, you can use a peacock or a rooster to symbolize the phoenix. Indeed, the Chinese believe all those born in a rooster year under the Chinese calendar have the potential to transform into the phoenix. This means that they achieve great fame and success and are highly respected and honored.

THE EIGHT ORDINARY SYMBOLS

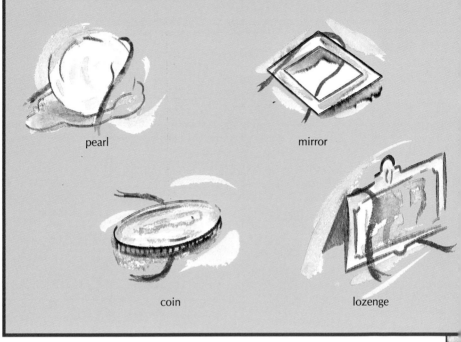

pearl

mirror

coin

lozenge

CLAIMING THE EIGHT TREASURES

To make the home auspicious, feng shui practitioners often claim the eight treasures by placing their symbols within the home and then activating their good qualities by tying them with red thread or placing them on a red tablecloth. There are several versions of these eight treasures and, unless one is well schooled in the classics and legends of ancient China, it is easy to become confused with the symbols. For feng shui purposes, it is sufficient to select the symbols from two versions.

The symbols are the dragon's pearl, the golden coin, the mirror, two books, the artemesia leaf, the stone chime, the rhinoceros' horns, and the lozenge. It is not necessary to use every one of them. The golden coin is a favorite "treasure" for using in this way since it also symbolizes wealth.

These good-luck symbols are believed to activate success luck within the home. Place one or all of them on a table in the living room in the corner that represents your success direction according to the Kua formula. Do not forget either to tie them with red thread or ribbon or to place a small piece of red cloth beneath them to activate their qualities.

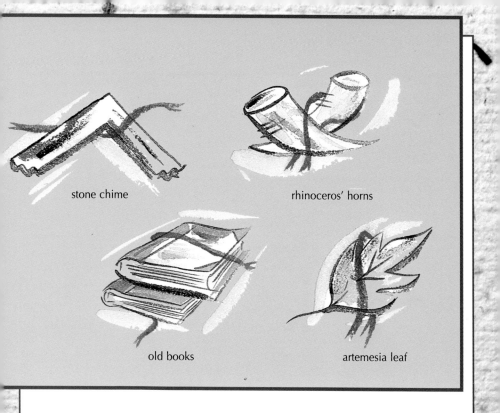

stone chime

rhinoceros' horns

old books

artemesia leaf

ACTIVATING THE COIN

Although you can use any coin to symbolize the good fortune of wealth, I always recommend using old Chinese coins which are round with a square hole in the center, symbolizing the unity of heaven and earth. In addition, the two sides of the coin symbolize yin and yang. The side with two characters is said to be the yin side, while the other with the four characters is said to be the yang side. For feng shui purposes, it is advisable to tie three of these old coins with a red thread and then place them, yang side up, in your auspicious corner. The coins can be hung, stuck onto the wall, or placed on the table top.

ACTIVATING THE DRAGON'S PEARL

The pearl is supposed to be the elusive essence of the moon goddess, and is said to act as a charm against too much fire. Thus it guards against the over-ambition that brings arrogance and the downfall of even the most powerful.

The pearl is also an emblem of genius, purity, and beauty. Generally, anything round or spherical can be said to represent the pearl. A ceramic model of the celestial dragon holding the pearl can be displayed on the dragon side of the home – the east – in order to attract good fortune luck to all the women of the family.

THE EIGHT AUSPICIOUS SYMBOLS

These eight symbols are believed to have appeared on the sole of the Buddha's foot. They are exceedingly popular among the Chinese who follow the Buddhist faith and are regarded with great respect. The eight symbols are the wheel, the conch shell, the umbrella, the canopy or flag, the lotus, the jar, the fish, and the mystic knot. These symbols can usually be seen in Chinese emporiums, particularly the fish, which is probably the most popular of the eight.

Legend tells us that images of the wheel, canopy, umbrella, fish, jar, conch shell, lotus, and mystic knot were revealed on Buddha's foot.

THE WHEEL

This is the symbol of a person whose conduct is honorable and upright. It represents authority and power achieved. It is sometimes replaced by the bell. Place it in your lucky direction and tie a red thread to activate it.

THE CANOPY

The canopy or flag is usually desorated with auspicious words or symbols and then hung in the breeze. It is believed that each time the breeze blows it activates the auspicious energy and good luck symbolized by the good fortune symbol placed on the flag. Usually canopies made of red-colored material are believed to bring good fortune.

THE UMBRELLA

This is an ancient emblem of dignity and high rank; in the old days, high officials were often presented with umbrellas to signify respect. This is also the emblem held by one of the four legendary kings, Mo Li Hung, the guardian of the south. Place an umbrella in the south corner of your home to signify protection from loss of name.

THE FISH

This is always symbolically applied as an emblem of wealth, mainly because phonetically the word fish in Chinese sounds like abundance. The sign of the double fish symbolizes happiness. Placing the symbol of the fish in the home signifies the successful attainment of one's goals.

THE JAR

A decorative jar, filled to the brim with water and placed near the entrance to the home is believed to symbolize great good fortune. Remember to keep the water fresh by changing it regularly, and keep a sense of balance by matching the size of the jar to the size of your home.

THE CONCH SHELL

In the old days, this was a royal insignia, often used as a symbol to represent a prosperous voyage. It is supposed to attract excellent fame luck when mounted on a rosewood stand and displayed in the lucky corner of your home. In ancient times, the conch shell was also used as a trumpet, so it signifies your name being known far and wide.

THE LOTUS

This is one of the most popular emblems, signifying great achievements from the humblest beginnings, like a magnificent bloom rising out of muddy waters. The lotus is also symbolic of summer. Incorporate this motif into your soft furnishings if you wish to introduce this good-fortune symbol into your home.

THE MYSTIC KNOT

This knot represents many things, including longevity, as it is endless, and love, because it has no beginning and no end.

The knot also represents the attainment of immortality for one's name. Feng shui Masters take their cue from the motifs seen in the palaces of the Forbidden City in Beijing and recommend the use of the knot to symbolize its attributes within the home.

DRUMS, TRUMPETS, BELLS, AND WINDCHIMES

These symbols, which create sounds, are extremely useful for attracting the luck of fame and success into the home. Sounds also create yang energy. By themselves such symbols do not necessarily have the potency of the compass orientations. They are, however, excellent supplements to the Kua formula and the use of the eight treasures.

Drums and trumpets herald the coming of auspicious developments. If you have a musical family and these objects are present in your home, keep

The trumpet belongs to the metal element, and if played in the south part of the house, it will activate fame luck.

them in a room in the south part of the house or in the corner that represents your success direction. If possible, do your music practice in these rooms to help activate fame luck.

Bells and windchimes are objects that usually belong to the metal element and so are controlled by the fire element. Their sounds are very welcome in the south as well. They can be placed in the south part of the home or the south part of the family or living room. When using these objects to activate your personal success corner, however, it is necessary to be careful. Bells and windchimes should not be placed in the wood corners – east and southeast – because metal destroys wood. Therefore, if these happen to be your success directions, it is far better not to use these objects.

Drums create a lot of yang energy and herald auspicious events.

WINDCHIMES

These are also very useful for overcoming common feng shui problems encountered in any home. Hang them when a particularly threatening, exposed, overhead beam runs across your working desk, dining table, or living room. I am not keen on placing windchimes in the bedroom, since it is not advisable to activate too much yang energy there.

A windchime effectively deflects the bad feng shui of the overhead beam.

A windchime hung above the second door, when there are three doors in a row, deflects the bad feng shui of this feature,

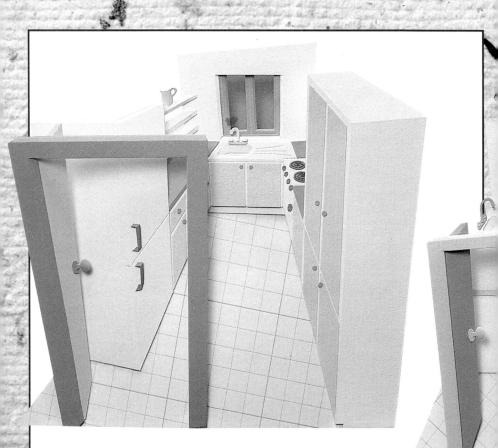

This kitchen is badly arranged
in terms of feng shui and will prove
damaging to the family's prosperity
and well-being.

PLACEMENT OF THE COOKER

Reputations can be substantially hurt when there are problems with the cooker location. Feng shui strenuously warns successful men and women always to take good care of their cookers (or rice cookers if their staple food is rice). This is because fame and reputation luck are very vulnerable if the cooker is placed in the wrong position or facing the wrong direction.

ORIENTATION OF THE COOKER

The cooker should have its source of energy coming from the direction that represents your personal success direction. If this is not possible, try to tap one of the other three directions that belong to your group of directions. Try at all costs to avoid having the cooker get its energy from any one of your four inauspicious directions, as this could lead to lawsuits, scandals, and a fall from grace.

This kitchen has the furniture and equipment arranged so that the chi can flow through freely, and there are no clashing elements.

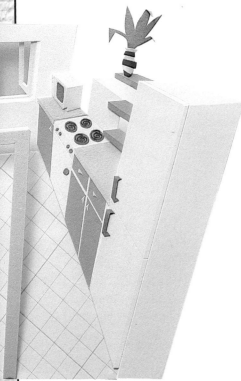

- The cooker should not face the main door.
- The cooker should not face the toilet or bathroom door.
- The cooker should not face the master bedroom door.
- The cooker should not be located directly under a beam.
- The cooker should not directly face a staircase.
- The cooker should not be in the northwest of the kitchen.
- The cooker should never be placed awkwardly or in a corner.
- The cooker should not be sandwiched between two sinks or taps. This symbolizes tears within the family, caused by a severe misfortune or loss.

TAKE CARE

The energies created by the cooker are extremely strong. It is thus advisable to be careful that these energies do not hurt the important areas of the home. In feng shui, however, it is not always possible to get everything right. So where a choice has to be made between different options, always choose to protect the main door.

Feng Shui
Fundamentals

Health

FENG SHUI FOR HEALTH

THE DIRECTION EAST

Chen is the growth trigram that represents good health. According to the Later Heaven Arrangement, it is placed in the east. This is the corner of any home or room that represents good health for the family.

If this corner has good feng shui, family members, especially the bread-winner, will enjoy excellent health and live to a ripe old age. If this corner has bad feng shui, illnesses will befall the family.

THE WOOD ELEMENT

The element of the east corner is wood, symbolized mainly by plants. Identifying the relevant element to

THE TREE OF LIFE

Reminiscent of other cultures, the Tree of Life is often depicted on carpets. This would be a suitable object to place in the east to symbolize the trigram Chen.

activate is a vital part of the application. It suggests that placing a healthy plant in the east will activate excellent health luck for residents of the home.

- ▨ Wood is produced by water, so water is said to be good for it.
- ▨ Wood itself produces fire, so fire will exhaust it.
- ▨ Wood is destroyed by metal, so metal will be harmful to it.
- ▨ Wood destroys earth, so earth is overcome by it.

From these attributes we know that to strengthen the element of the east, we can use all objects that symbolize both wood and water, but should strenuously avoid anything belonging to the metal element. Delving deeper, we see that the east is represented by big wood. This suggests that the intangible forces of the wood in this corner are strong, powerful, and not easily overcome. Big wood is suggestive of very strong growth.

Wood is the only one of the five elements that is alive and capable of reproducing itself. This implies that the yang energies of its corner, although not immediately evident, are nevertheless strong. This is eloquently suggested by the lines of the trigram where the unbroken yang line lies hidden under two yin lines. Using inanimate objects made of wood can thus be equally effective as using plants for energizing this corner of the home.

CHEN

This trigram represents the eldest son. It has two yin lines above a single unbroken yang line. Chen also signifies spring, which is a season of growth. In the language of the ancient Chinese text, the I Ching, Chen stands for the "arousing", characterized by great claps of thunder bursting in the spring sky, waking creatures from hibernation, and causing the life-giving rains to fall. Chen is a happy trigram that also suggests laughter and happiness. It has great strength and energy.

That it stands for growth and vigor is what makes it representative of life itself. Activating the corner that houses this trigram attracts healthy growth energies. The direction is east and the element is big wood, suggestive of trees rather than bushes, a deep green color rather than light green, and large wooden structures (furniture) rather than small wooden objects (ornaments).

ENERGIZING THE WOOD ELEMENT

Each of the five elements is activated by the presence of objects belonging to the same group. Plants, especially healthy-growing plants that look green, lush, and well cared for, are probably the best symbols to use to stimulate the wood element of the east health corner.

If you are fortunate enough to have land around your home, try growing a clump of bamboo in the east corner of your garden. Bamboo is one of the most popular Chinese symbols of longevity and strength. Any variety is fine, but keep the bamboo well cultivated from season to season.

Plant a window box of flowering plants if there is a window in the east corner of the room you wish to activate. This will attract healthy yang energy into the room.

These should ideally be living plants, although realistic-looking silk or other artificial plants are also quite effective. It is important to avoid using dried plants or artificial plants that look dead or have gathered so much dust that they suggest a sad stagnation of energies. Artificial plants that depict a plant in winter are also ineffective. The idea is to symbolize healthily growing plants – the way they look in spring.

You can also place a small plant on a table top in the east corner if the room is small. In feng shui always be aware of the need for balance. Activating any element should not be overdone. Thus plants placed in a room should never seem to overwhelm it.

If there is an edge in the east part of the room being activated, caused by a protruding corner, a square pillar, or a piece of furniture, place a plant, such as the one shown here, against it. This not only serves to deflect the harmful energies created by the sharp edge, but also simultaneously stimulates the vibrancy of the wood element. Over time, the plant may lose its vigor and even wilt and die. If so, throw it out and place a fresh, new plant there.

INDIVIDUAL HEALTH DIRECTIONS

THE COMPASS FORMULA

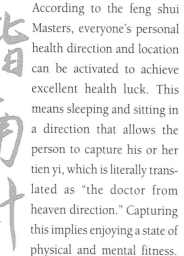

According to the feng shui Masters, everyone's personal health direction and location can be activated to achieve excellent health luck. This means sleeping and sitting in a direction that allows the person to capture his or her tien yi, which is literally translated as "the doctor from heaven direction." Capturing this implies enjoying a state of physical and mental fitness. This formula is ideal for people who are constantly tired and lethargic, and also helps alleviate those suffering from illness, although the focus of feng shui practice is on prevention rather than cure.

THE CHINESE PERSPECTIVE ON HEALTH AND LONGEVITY

Longevity and a life of good health have preoccupied the Chinese since time immemorial. Chinese traditional practice is replete with doctrines and techniques to address this aspect of human life. The search was once for immortality. Through the centuries this gave way to more realistic goals and eventually techniques were developed that could be practiced to lengthen the lifespan. These techniques drew on the Chinese abstraction of chi. If the human chi was strong and balanced, the health of the physical body

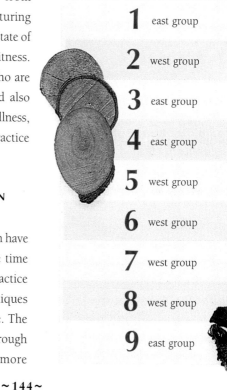

If your Kua number is:

1 east group

2 west group

3 east group

4 east group

5 west group

6 west group

7 west group

8 west group

9 east group

would be excellent, but if the chi was blocked, it would cause sickness. When chi was extinguished altogether, it resulted in death. In addition, when total harmony existed between the environmental and human chi, a long happy life was believed to result. Thus the Chinese have developed movements aimed at encouraging the harmonious flow of chi in the body and at exercising the five vital internal organs (see overleaf).

Your Health orientation is:

NORTH for both males and females

SOUTHWEST for both males and females

EAST for both males and females

SOUTHEAST for both males and females

SOUTHWEST for males and
NORTHEAST for females

NORTHWEST for both males and females

WEST for both males and females

NORTHEAST for both males and females

SOUTH for both males and females

THE KUA FORMULA

Add the last two digits of your Chinese year of birth. e.g. **1956, 5+6=11**.
If the sum is higher than ten, reduce to a single digit; thus **1+1=2**.

Males	Females
Subtract from	Add
10	**5**
thus	thus
10-2	**5+2**
=8	**=7**
So, for men born in	So, for women born in
1956	**1956**
the Kua number is	the Kua number is
8	**7**

There is no number 5 in this system, although it is included here for clarity. Females should use 8 instead of 5, and males 2.

THE CELESTIAL ANIMALS HEALTH EXERCISES

Orientating your home according to the principles of feng shui can be effectively supplemented with the simple health exercises developed by the Shaolin and Tai Chi Masters. The movements of these exercises were designed to allow the human body to create the vital breath, termed chi. Many of these are very simple exercises and they are named after the celestial animals, the dragon, tiger, phoenix, and turtle, and for the longevity creatures, the deer and crane. The Turtle Exercise falls into both categories, and is featured on page 151.

Anyone can use these exercises to maintain balanced physical and emotional states. However, if there is a specific problem affecting an internal organ, select the appropriate exercise according to the five elements theory to bring healing energies to the particular afflicted organ. The heart is of the fire element, the lungs metal, the liver wood, and the spleen and stomach are of the earth element.

This exercise addresses the fire element and is excellent for creating healing energies in the spleen, stomach, and all the muscles of the body. These represent the earth element. The exercise also helps overcome feelings of anger, anxiety, and hostility, and strengthens the heart. The method is free-form and relaxed. Hold the pose as long as you can and repeat several times.

The recommended time is half an hour each morning. You will feel your palms

This is the second stage of the dragon exercise. It is also excellent for firing your ambitions and motivating you, but in a very relaxed, non-stressful way. The method is very simple and involves cycles of breathing. Do nine cycles.

1. Stand still, facing east, and think of the dragon. Bend your knees slightly and hold your navel with both hands, keeping your spine straight and your tail bone tucked in.

THE RELAXED DRAGON EXERCISE

1. Stand still with feet as far apart as your shoulders. Take a few deep breaths and visualize yourself as a dragon.

2. Bend your knees very slightly, keep your spine straight and pull your tail bone in. Let your arms hang loosely by your sides, with palms facing inward. Breathe normally, let the mouth relax and keep the tongue gently touching the top of the palate. Stand like this for as long as you can.

tingle slightly and, after about ten minutes, you will feel the chi moving up your hands. With time and practice the chi will move down into the tạn tien, in the navel area, where it is believed all human chi is stored. This exercise is the first stage exercise of many different types of Chinese martial arts.

THE BREATHING DRAGON EXERCISE

2. With your left hand on your stomach and the right palm covering the left hand, breathe in through your nose and feel the breath going into the stomach. Do this very slowly!

3. Feel the stomach expand like a drum or a balloon.

4. When you cannot breathe in any longer, bend forward 15–25 degrees and breathe out slowly at the same speed that you inhaled. Breath out until your stomach feels hollow. Straighten. This is one cycle of breath.

THE FLYING PHOENIX EXERCISE

This exercise is associated with the metal element and is useful in overcoming melancholia and depression, which, if not addressed, could lead to lung problems. The phoenix is said to have the ability to rise from the ashes and soar effortlessly to great heights. This exercise cheers the soul considerably – be aware of the chi moving as you do it. This is a wonderful exercise and you will feel your palms tingle within a few minutes. This is the chi slowly gathering energy in your palms before moving inward and filling you with a sense of well-being. The recommended time for holding this pose is about 15 minutes each morning.

1. Stand still, keeping the spine straight, the tailbone tucked in, with your feet apart and the knees slightly bent. Imagine yourself as a phoenix.

2. Extend your arms horizontally outward, as if spreading your wings ready to fly.

3. Keeping your arms flexed, gently raise your hands to form a right-angle. Keep your palms facing outward, absorbing the chi of the surroundings. Let your tongue rest gently at the top of your mouth and hold this pose for as long as you can.

THE CRANE

The red-combed crane is a popular symbol of longevity and the ancients believe it was the bird's unique pose – standing on one leg, with the other folded into its belly – that gave it the ability to survive on all kinds of diets. They were convinced that the pose stimulated its stomach and internal organs, thereby strengthening the digestive, respiratory, and circulatory systems. So, the exercise, involves standing on one leg.

THE HAPPY PHOENIX EXERCISE

This is also referred to as the one-hundred year movement or pak sau kung. This exercise is believed to be so good for heath, those who do it faithfully each morning will live to be 100 years old! It is very simple exercise and takes only ten minutes to do.

1. Stand straight with your left leg half a pace in front of the right. and your feet apart the same width as your shoulders.

2. With the knees slightly bent, the spine straight, and the tail bone tucked in, extend both arms straight in front, palms down.

3. Bend forward and down slowly to about 20 degrees, with the spine still straight (not curved). At the same time, allow your arms to swing back rather like preparing to dive into a pool. Look down as you bend forward.

4. Straighten. Do this movement nine times.

XERCISE

1. Stand with the feet together with toes and heels touching. Place the sole of one foot on the calf of the other leg.

2. Slowly work the foot up to the inner thigh. Then slowly raise both hands above your head, inhaling as you do so. Join your hands and hold this position as long as you can.

THE MAGICAL TURTLE

The turtle is one of the four celestial animals in feng shui cosmology. Together with the green dragon, the white tiger, and the crimson phoenix, the black turtle is part of the important quartet that symbolically defines excellent landscape feng shui. Like the other creatures, the turtle is an important feng shui tool.

The turtle is also very important for its role in bringing the Lo Shu square to the world. An old Chinese legend describes how the numbers of the square were brought to humankind on the back of a turtle that emerged from the River Lo many thousands of years ago. The Lo Shu square is the tool that unlocked the secrets of the Pa Kua symbol.

The turtle symbolizes several wonderful aspects of good fortune that make life pleasant, but its most outstanding attribute is as a symbol of longevity. There is a wonderful legend about the turtle that describes how, with a minimum of movement, it conserves its energy, reduces its need for sustenance, and lives to a thousand years old.

The turtle also symbolizes support. Its direction is actually the north and the element associated with it is water. This makes its presence in the east sector, the corner that represents good health, extremely compatible. Place a model of a turtle in the east if you want to benefit from the wonderful good-health energies that its presence brings to the home.

TURTLES AND TURTLE SUBSTITUTES

Turtles are frequently used to activate good feng shui.
If turtles are not easy to come by, it is just as acceptable to put a tank of terrapins in the east corner. Remember that feng shui places great emphasis on symbolism, so even a painting or a print of a turtle would be effective.

THE TURTLE EXERCISE

1. Relax and then bring your chin down on to your chest.

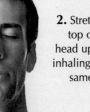

2. Stretch the top of your head upward, inhaling at the same time.

3. Bring your head further back, while simultaneously exhaling.

Repeat eight times.

Legend tells of a turtle that lived deep in a cave with a family who had been trapped there during a landslide. The family, it is said, survived for 800 years by emulating the turtle's minimal movements. Indeed, they discovered that virtually the only movement the turtle made was to extend and retract its head in and out of its shell. Occasionally, it would extend its tongue to catch a drop of water from the ceiling of the cave. By copying the turtle, the family survived through the centuries, their story spread, and soon became a legend.

From the story came the Turtle Exercise, which is incorporated in many Chinese health systems. It may be done sitting or standing.

SLEEPING ORIENTATIONS AFFECT HEALTH

THE LOCATION OF YOUR BEDROOM

睡
眠

While the Kua formula prescribes the ideal location for your bedroom according to specific compass directions, you must also take account of other factors. Thus, irrespective of where the bedroom is actually located in the home, there are certain guidelines that should be strictly observed to safeguard your health. Much of this has to do with ensuring that you are not attacked by what feng shui Masters refer to as the killing breath; unfriendly energies that bring illness, bad temper, and depression.

Bedrooms located at the end of a long corridor cause ill-health because the flow of energy is too strong, especially if the door into the bedroom is placed at the end of the corridor, as shown on the facing page. The situation becomes worse if there is also a door at the other end of the corridor or if the bed inside the bedroom is placed with the feet of the sleeper directly facing the door. Breaking any one of these guidelines attracts health problems for the occupant of the bedroom, and sometimes the energies created can be so strong, the effect is overwhelming. The way to deal with such a situation is to change the placement of the bed.

The energy in bedrooms located in a part of the building that gets no sunlight at all, or where there are virtually no windows, is said to be too yin. The lack of sunshine and fresh air will make the air stale and the chi becomes stagnant. Bedrooms should be regularly aired and well lit or the consequence will be a build-up of bad chi that manifests itself first in illness, then in other forms of bad luck that follow.

Bedrooms located in a basement, or on a lower floor directly below a toilet, washing machine, or cooker on the upper floor are considered inauspicious. Bad, harmful chi is created on a daily basis and affects the health of the people sleeping below. The worst situation is for a person to sleep beneath a toilet. Avoid this at all costs.

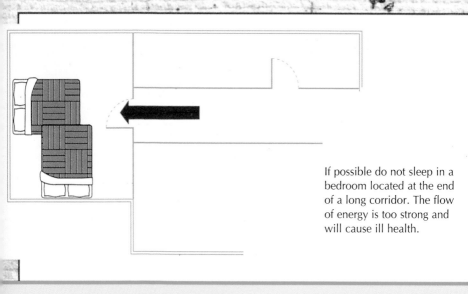

If possible do not sleep in a bedroom located at the end of a long corridor. The flow of energy is too strong and will cause ill health.

POSITIONING YOUR BED

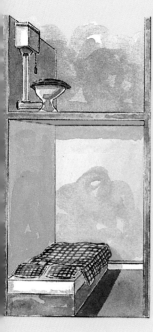

Avoid sleeping beneath a toilet.

Harmful chi will affect a person sleeping beneath a washing machine.

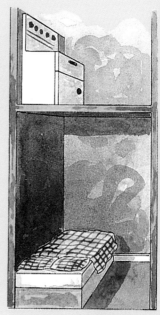

It is considered inauspicious to sleep below a cooker.

THE POSITION AND ORIENTATION OF THE BED

Make sure your bed is located in an auspicious place according to form school feng shui before attempting to tap your best health direction. It is always advisable to start out by first protecting yourself from what feng shui practitioners term hidden poison arrows. Watch out for any offensive features or structures that may inadvertently be sending poison arrows of bad chi toward you as you sleep. These cause headaches, migraines, and other forms of illness. Focus on the placement of the bed inside the room itself.

The arrow in the illustration shows you how to take the direction in the correct way. Note that the head should be pointed in the auspicious direction. If you and your partner have different auspicious directions, sleep in two separate beds. Note that the bed is placed diagonally to the door. This is the best placement from a feng shui perspective.

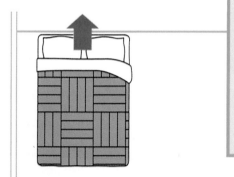

PRACTICAL GUIDEL·INES

To safeguard the harmony of the home, the position of the bedrooms in the overall layout is also important. Try to select a bedroom that does not have any of the following features and also to observe some of these practical guidelines.

- Try to ensure that the bedroom door does not open directly to a toilet. Nor should the bed be placed against a wall that is shared by a toilet.
- Try to avoid having a bedroom door that opens directly on to a staircase, as this causes unfortunate chi to enter the bedroom, hurting the occupant.
- Try not to have the bedroom door directly face the corner edge of another room. This causes a blockage of chi, resulting in circulatory ailments for the occupant of the room.
- If a room has previously been occupied by someone very ill, it is a good idea to give it a good airing before allocating it to someone else. Install a bright light, paint the room a bright, happy colour and turn on the music. This re-introduces much-needed yang energy.

EXAMPLES OF HARMFUL BED PLACEMENT

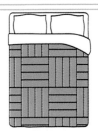

A bed that is placed directly in front of a door will suffer from bad chi.

The sharp edge of the protruding corner is sending a poison arrow toward the bed. Move the bed or camouflage the offensive corner.

The bed is placed just below a window. It is also being affected by the door to the attached toilet. These are both inauspicious features. The bed should be moved and placed in the opposite corner.

Living next to a prison, hospital, or cemetery can often cause residents to suffer from illness caused by an excess of yin energies.

DEALING WITH ENERGIES THAT ARE TOO YIN

The physical well-being of residents is often affected and they succumb more easily to illness when the energies that surround their home are too yin. The theory of feng shui always requires there to be a harmonious balance of yin and yang energies. When there is too much yin energy, health suffers; often more so than when there is too much yang energy. This is because yin is representative of death, while yang is symbolic of life.

Yin energies are considered to be much too strong and overwhelming when your home is located in the vicinity of a police station, cemetery, hospital, slaughterhouse, or any other place associated with despair, death, and illness. It is worse if your home is situated right next to any of these places. Some feng shui practitioners go so far as to investigate the history of the land where a new home is to be sited or the previous use of buildings that are to be converted into residential apartments. Feng shui contends that the energies of previous occupants linger and when these are sickly or weak, the energies are very yin. Consequently, if your home is located on a site that formerly housed a hospital or a prison, indications will be that the place is too yin, often to a harmful extent..

If you have a choice, it is advisable not to have a home near such places. Otherwise, the way to deal with excessive yin energy is to introduce healthy doses of yang energy.

ROOMS THAT ARE TOO YIN

A room that is excessively yin is one that has previously been occupied by someone very ill, that has no windows, or has not been cleaned for several years so the energies within have been allowed to grow stale and stagnant. If you move into such a room, then even if you sleep with your head pointed in your health direction, you will succumb to the bad energies. In this case, repaint the room or clear out the stagnant energy by giving it a good scrub and installing bright lights. Then play some music in there to liven up the atmosphere.

PLAY MUSIC

Sounds, especially happy ones, are a wonderful antidote to excessive yin energy. Keep the radio or television playing the entire day, even when you are not at home, and especially if you are living by yourself. Sounds activate the living space and clear out stale, stagnant energies.

Keep the area just outside your main door brightly lit at all times. The bright light is symbolic of powerful yang energy and is most effective in ensuring a more auspicious balance of yin and yang. Spotlights are ideal, but porch lights are just as effective. Paint your main front door a bright, happy red. This is a most effective way of countering excessive yin energy and could even bring better luck.

COUNTERACTING
STALE AND STAGNANT ENERGY

When the energies around and within a home become stale and stagnant, the health of the residents suffers. This is regarded as one of the most common causes of poor health. People constantly succumb to the common cold, stomach ulcers, and other ailments.

Stale chi is principally created when the air within the home has not been cleared out. During dark winter days, when windows stay closed for long periods, it is easy for the chi inside the home to stagnate. If there is also clutter and dirt, the situation is seriously compounded. This is because winter is also the cold season of yin, when yang energy is in short supply. A preponderance of yin energy at this time of year can therefore lead to illness, lethargy, and even depression.

Keeping the home well heated and well lit creates healthy yang energy. Of course, it also creates much-needed warmth. More importantly, it causes energies to become balanced and fresh. Playing lively music also generates happy chi. This is why it is always a good idea to have a Christmas tree in the house. Decorating the tree with sparkling ornaments and lights will ensure that wonderful healthy chi is created. Beautiful and inspiring choral music will also add happy chi to the living space.

All the symbols and decorations of the Christmas season bring healthy yang energy – candles, lights, bells, red ribbons, colorful ornaments hung on brightly lit trees. It is the same with the seasonal celebrations or festivals of most other cultures.

'SPRING' CLEANING

Perhaps it is a subconscious need to clean up the home to clear its energies that has led peoples of all backgrounds and cultures to undertake a thorough cleaning prior to celebrating traditional happy occasions – although not only in the spring. As it is for Jews celebrating Passover, so it is, too, for the Chinese celebrating the lunar New Year and for the Muslims celebrating Eid al-Fitr after a month of fasting during Ramadan, a practice that is believed to cleanse the body and the mind. Almost all traditional happy occasions are times when lights are used lavishly. The people of the Indian subcontinent, for example, celebrate Diwali, also known as the Festival of Lights.

To enjoy healthy feng shui in your living space, it is vital that the home be kept clean and free of clutter. Blocked

The use of lights at times of celebration, like the candles lit by these Buddhists in Shanghai, fills the air with healthy chi.

drains should be cleared. Plumbing represents the arteries of the home, and any blockage can cause serious illness when not attended to. Appliances that have broken down should be repaired. You should get rid of polluted or dirty water in the garden and if the toilet or bathroom become clogged, the problem should be attended to immediately. All of this may seem to be good sound common sense, but it is surprising how often simple repair chores are put off. From a feng shui point of view, this is unhealthy.

Clear any blockages in your plumbing system.

Feng Shui
Fundamentals

Children

FENG SHUI FOR THE
NEXT GENERATION

ENERGIZING THE PA KUA
FOR CHILDREN'S LUCK

Using feng shui to activate your children's luck will result in a happy and creative atmosphere.

Activating your children's luck starts with understanding the Pa Kua. By itself, the Pa Kua of the Early Heaven Arrangement is believed to be a powerful protective tool. Merely hanging it outside the home above the main door is deemed very effective in countering any negative energies that may be threatening the home and its residents.

However, the Pa Kua, with its aggregated circles of meaning, is also a feng shui reference tool. There is meaning in each of the trigrams placed at every edge of it. Trigrams are three-lined symbols. The lines may be solid yang or broken yin lines and their relationship is what gives meaning to the trigrams, according to the I Ching, the Book of Changes.

The trigram that represents the next generation is Tui and, according to the Later Heaven Arrangement, this is placed in the west. This is the corner of any home or room that represents the luck of the children. If this corner has good feng shui, the children will enjoy excellent fortune: they will do well in school, achieve good grades, win honors, and excel in all their pursuits. If they enjoy good birth charts, the good feng shui will also assist them in attaining great heights in any endeavor.

However, if this corner has bad feng shui, bad luck will prevail and parents will find it difficult to help their children. The children themselves will suffer from every kind of misfortune, from not doing well

TUI

This trigram, made up of one broken yin line above two unbroken yang lines, signifies joyousness, laughter, and a time for rejoicing. The Tui trigram implies success and continuity of the family name. Seasonally, it represents fall and its symbol is the lake.

More than anything, Tui means gold, but not ordinary gold. The reference is metaphorical, for gold here means virtuous offspring who bring fame, honor, and happiness to the family. Good children are regarded as being as precious as gold. When the trigram Tui is activated, there is harmony in the family. Siblings enjoy good relationships and children respect the elders of the family. Husbands and wives get along and the atmosphere in the home is one of serenity.

The positive side of this trigram also suggests that families will be enlarged through marriage or having children.

at school to constantly falling sick. They will find it difficult and sometimes impossible to achieve their potential despite their best efforts.

In order to maximize children's luck, feng shui requires careful examination of this sector of the room or home and in particular the meaning of the trigram Tui.

COMPASS DIRECTIONS AND ELEMENTS

THE CYCLES OF THE FIVE ELEMENTS

Applying element analysis to feng shui practice requires an understanding of the nature of their interactions with each other. According to the theory, there are two cycles that form the basis of element interpretation. These are the productive and the destructive cycles. The five elements interact with each other and move in never-ending positive and negative cycles.

The universal corner identified with children's luck is the west for which the element is metal. The northern Chinese schools of feng shui, however, also consider the east beneficial for children, since this is the family luck corner. The element of the east is wood.

PRODUCTIVE CYCLE

LUCK

One method of activating luck for the children of the family requires the following three steps

▨ Identify the corner of the home and its rooms that represent children.

▨ Check the corresponding element of the corner(s) identified.

▨ Activate the corner using elements as a guide.

DESTRUCTIVE CYCLE

This illustration shows the destructive cycle of the five elements. Metal is being overwhelmed by fire, the element that destroys metal. This means that metal, which is associated with children's luck, is not being strengthened.

THE METAL ELEMENT OF THE WEST

The ruling element of the west is metal, symbolized by all things made of metal, particularly gold. This includes metal windchimes, home appliances, televisions, and clocks. Identifying the relevant element to activate is a vital part of feng shui application. For instance, a windchime in the west part of the living room will activate excellent opportunities for the children of the family.

From these attributes, we know that to strengthen the element of the west, we can use any objects that symbolize either earth or metal elements, but that we should avoid anything belonging to the fire element. This means that the west may be activated by any object, color, or painting that suggests either earth or metal. Electrical appliances that are made of metal and are placed in the west corner of a room would be harmonious. The display of windchimes and bells is also excellent, as are television sets and music systems. It is also auspicious to display objects that belong to the earth element, such as crystals, clay pots, and rocks.

METAL

Examination of five element cycles reveals various characteristics of the metal element.

- Metal is produced by earth, so earth is said to be good for it.
- Metal itself produces water, so water is said to exhaust it.
- Metal is destroyed by fire, so fire is said to be harmful to it.
- Metal destroys wood, so it is said to overcome wood.

USING OBJECTS OF
THE METAL ELEMENT

Energizing the west is said to enhance the life force that brings auspicious benefits to children. Placing metal objects in the west of any room, or in the room which represents the west corner of the home, attracts the beneficial sheng chi that ensures children do well in their studies and careers. In practical feng shui this means placing household objects and appliances according to feng shui principles and incorporating the attributes and symbols of the metal element into the decoration of the room.

Display the family silver in a glass-fronted cabinet placed against the west wall of the living room, set up the television or stereo system there, or hang a clock on that wall. You can set up the computer terminal in the west corner of the study. Make sure the wall that represents this direction is painted white, since this is the color that symbolizes metal.

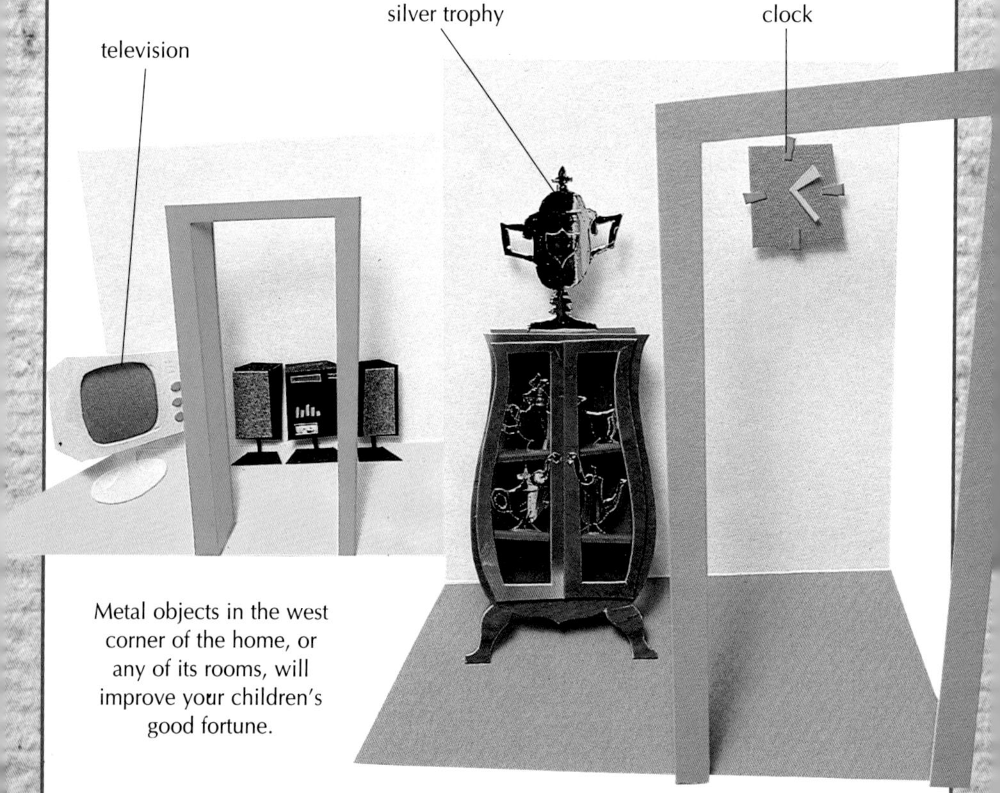

television

silver trophy

clock

Metal objects in the west corner of the home, or any of its rooms, will improve your children's good fortune.

USING OBJECTS WITH ADDITIONAL FENG SHUI SIGNIFICANCE

The sound of bells attract good sheng chi and activate your children's luck.

There are other objects that have greater feng shui significance. Perhaps one of the most effective feng shui energizers is a windchime that is made of metal. A bell is another favorite object of good fortune, deemed most suitable for activating auspicious children's luck. The Chinese place dragon bells on the west side of their rooms to summon the family to dinner. Bells are also considered good feng shui because their sound attracts the good sheng chi. Any kind of bell is acceptable, but it is a good idea to look for decorative ones made of brass, which emit attractive sounds that bring good feng shui. Bells are also excellent energizers when hung on the door handles of main doors. This is also believed to enhance business luck.

THE WINDCHIME

Made of several hollow rods tied together, the windchime is said to be very effective in channeling sheng chi upwards. The tinkling sounds of the rods as they move in the wind are said to encourage the auspicious life force to accumulate and settle, bringing good fortune to the household. Windchimes with solid rods are ineffective as feng shui energizers. In Chinese homes, windchimes made of copper and fashioned into pagodas and stars are very popular because the Chinese also believe that the windchime by itself is an auspicious object to have in the home. Place the chime in the west to create good luck for the children, but do not overdo it. One windchime is sufficient.

THE WOOD ELEMENT OF THE EAST

The symbolic element of the east is wood and the best representation of it is living plants and flowers. Since east is regarded as the corner that affects family luck, activating east walls, corners, and even the roof will attract precious sheng chi to the home – the sort that brings happiness and luck to the children of the family. Their success and well-being will be improved vastly and there will be more respect from the children for their parents, and better communication from everyone.

When energizing wood, you should consider the attributes of this element in relation to the others.

▨ Wood is produced by water, so water is said to be good for it.
▨ Wood itself produces fire, so fire is said to exhaust it.
▨ Wood is destroyed by metal, so metal is said to be harmful to it.
▨ Wood destroys earth, so it is said to overcome earth.

These relationships indicate that the east can, in effect, be energized by objects that belong to both the wood and water elements. It also suggests that placing objects of the metal element in the east, such as televisions or computers, or even windchimes, will destroy the intrinsic forces of the corner with disastrous results.

CACTUS AND BONSAI

Cactus and bonsai plants should be avoided. No matter how stunning they may look, resist the temptation to have them in your home, let alone in the east corner.

It is an excellent idea to combine the wood and water elements. Display a bowl of water lilies or place freshly cut flowers in a vase. Fresh flowers are always excellent feng shui, as they represent life and wonderful yang energy (but throw them away as soon as they wilt or the energy will stagnate).

Cactus has thorns that emit harmful shar chi and bonsai represents stunted growth, an unwanted symbolism, especially for children.

ACTIVATING WOOD INSIDE THE HOME

This can be done by displaying indoor plants. Place them on window sills to catch the morning sun and make sure they look healthy and luscious. Dying and sickly plants are bad feng shui and they should be thrown out and immediately replaced with healthy ones. Artificial plants are acceptable although live plants are better. However, dried flowers emit too much yin energy and so they do not represent good feng shui.

The healthier and more luxuriant the plant looks, the better the feng shui is considered to be.

Plants with rounded leaves and plenty of foliage are better than those with pointed leaves.

COLORS AND
INTERIOR DECORATION

White and metallic colors are the ones to use for the west corners of rooms. Correct colors strengthen the element and create a good feng shui balance for the corner, benefiting the type of luck it signifies. This guideline is best followed in the family or living room, as these are the ones that are most in use.

Soft furnishings, such as drapes, rugs, and cushion covers, can be any color except red, since red is of the fire element and that destroys metal.

BLUES AND GREENS FOR THE EAST

The combination of the water and wood elements suggest blues and greens in all shades. Use light tones for the walls and let your creativity run riot for all the soft furnishings. Flowered designs on sofa covers and rugs are excellent. Avoid metallic colors, including silver and gold, since metal destroys wood. Also avoid geometric designs with sharp edges. Checks and stripes do not represent auspicious feng shui. Designs with pointed edges do the most harm.

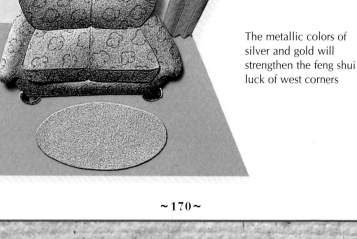

The metallic colors of silver and gold will strengthen the feng shui luck of west corners

MOTIFS AND DESIGNS

Wallpaper, drapes, rugs, and sofa covers can carry auspicious patterns that enhance the corners where they are placed. For the east, water, trees, flowers, or even the green dragon can be worked into designs. In the metal corners, motifs can incorporate gold or silver.

Rooms in the east should follow the elements of wood and water in their decoration. So blues and greens and floral decoration are all excellent.

COMPASS FENG SHUI FOR FAMILY LUCK

THE COMPASS FORMULA

The auspicious family direction of every person is known as the nien yen direction. Once you know your personal nien yen direction, you can make use of it to enhance your family luck through feng shui. You can use it with equal success in the various rooms of your home. Essentially this means sleeping and sitting in your auspicious direction, to attract excellent luck in your relations with all members of your family. In addition to benefiting your marriage and family happiness, this enhances your descendants-luck. Activating the nien yen of your children helps them focus.

THE CHINESE VIEW OF DESCENDANTS-LUCK

Luck with descendants has always been of such prime importance to the Chinese that feng shui merged strongly with superstition in the myriad beliefs and practices that address this universal aspiration of Chinese families. In the avenue of stone figures leading to the tombs of the Ming emperors just outside Beijing, there are gigantic stone monoliths of standing and kneeling elephants, which are believed to bring immeasurable descendants-luck to childless women. Placing a stone on the back of one of these elephants, it was believed, would ensure the birth of a male child. Indeed, references to offspring in the Chinese culture

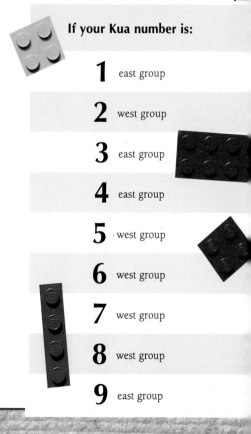

If your Kua number is:

1 east group

2 west group

3 east group

4 east group

5 west group

6 west group

7 west group

8 west group

9 east group

referred almost exclusively to sons. Even in modern China, sons are more welcome than daughters. Thus in the old textbooks on feng shui, luck was often described in terms of the number of sons a certain orientation would bring, and ill-luck in terms of the loss of sons.

Auspicious descendants-luck, however, also means that children will be filial, virtuous, and obedient – and Chinese folk tales are peppered with stories of filial devotion, duty, and obedience. Good feng shui can help ensure that families enjoy exactly this kind of good fortune.

THE KUA FORMULA

Calculate your Kua number as follows. Add the last two digits of your Chinese year of birth. e.g. **1957**, **5+7=12**.
If the sum is higher than ten, reduce to a single digit, thus **1+2=3**.

Males	Females
Subtract from	Add
10	**5**
thus	thus
10-3	**5+3**
=7	**=8**
So, for men born in	So, for women born in
1957	**1957**
the Kua number is	the Kua number is
7	**8**

Now check against this table for your family direction and location.

Your Family orientation is:

SOUTH for both males and females

NORTHWEST for both males and females

SOUTHEAST for both males and females

EAST for both males and females

NORTHWEST for males and **WEST** for females

SOUTHWEST for both males and females

NORTHEAST for both males and females

WEST for both males and females

NORTH for both males and females

IMPROVING SCHOOL GRADES

Perhaps the most exciting promise of feng shui is its potential to create living spaces that encourage and motivate children to perform to the best of their ability. Study skills and attitudes improve substantially when children work in a harmoniously balanced environment.

THE SITTING DIRECTION

The first thing to do is to position the work desk in a way that makes your child face his or her best study direction. Grades are almost certain to improve, and he or she will become far more motivated and focused in his or her studies. This method uses the Kua compass formula. Use your child's year of birth (adjusted to the Chinese calendar), and work out his or her Kua number according to the formula given on page 173, then check the best study direction from the table here. Whenever the child is working, he or she should sit facing the best study direction. It will enhance learning ability and memory because the surrounding energies will be harmonious and auspicious.

Your Kua number is:	Your Fu Wei orientation is:
1	**NORTH** for both males and females
2	**SOUTHWEST** for both males and females
3	**EAST** for both males and females
4	**SOUTHEAST** for both males and females
5	**SOUTHWEST** for males and **NORTHEAST** for females
6	**NORTHWEST** for both males and females
7	**WEST** for both males and females
8	**NORTHEAST** for both males and females
9	**SOUTH** for both males and females

Never let your child sit below a toilet located on the upper floor. Make certain nothing sharp or pointed, such as the edge of a closet or a protruding corner, is hitting at the chair where your child is working. This creates shar chi, which harms the child. Also make sure that there are no beams or edges above.

He or she should sit with the head facing the best study direction and solid support behind. A painting of a mountain is excellent. Do not position the desk so that the window is directly behind it; this symbolizes a lack of support.

This auspicious direction method can be applied in other situations. Let your child face this direction when doing his or her homework, when sitting for an examination, in class, or when revising if at all possible. It is important to remember, however, that the luck of the good direction is no protection against shar chi caused by beams, pillars, and sharp edges, so you must make sure that you always avoid these structures.

Finally, this direction can also be activated during mealtimes. Allocate seats at the family table according to the different auspicious directions of each of the children in the family.

HARMONY
AMONG SIBLINGS

ARRANGEMENT OF ROOMS

妹妹

How rooms are placed in relation to each other and how doors face each other has feng shui consequences. If they are placed correctly, siblings get along and there is goodwill between them. Where these have feng shui faults, it is much more likely that quarrels and misunderstandings will prevail.

A bedroom placed next to a toilet is seldom auspicious.

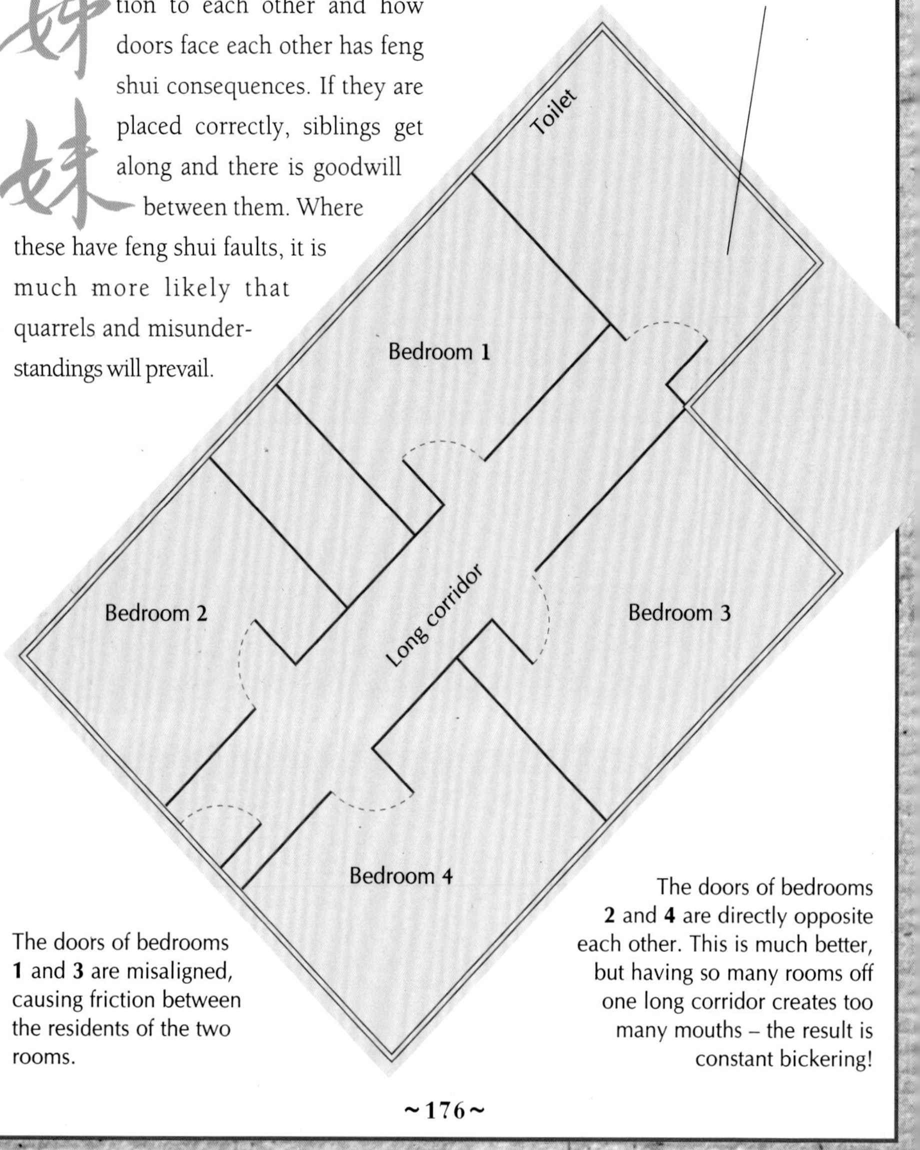

Toilet

Bedroom 1

Bedroom 2

Bedroom 3

Long corridor

Bedroom 4

The doors of bedrooms **1** and **3** are misaligned, causing friction between the residents of the two rooms.

The doors of bedrooms **2** and **4** are directly opposite each other. This is much better, but having so many rooms off one long corridor creates too many mouths – the result is constant bickering!

OTHER UNFORTUNATE ARRANGEMENTS

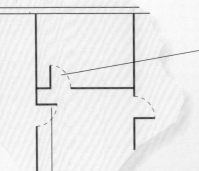

The hinges of this door have been fixed in a way that causes feng shui problems. Change the hinges, otherwise anyone occupying this room will be unable to get along with the rest of the household.

Doors should be the same size.

This door has been most awkwardly placed. It opens outward instead of inward. This indicates the occupant of this room cannot stay at home and cannot get along with his or her siblings. It is also blocking the other door, thereby affecting the feng shui of the occupant of the other room.

SIZE OF BEDS

Unlikely as this may seem, many parents allow their children to sleep on beds that are either far too large or small for their children. Tall children sleeping on beds that are too short will suffer from constant illness. Different size beds for different children causes hidden resentments and jealousies among siblings. Get beds that are in proportion to your children's physique and allow them room to grow.

SIZE OF DOORS

Doors that are next to, or near, each other should be of the same dimensions. If one is larger or taller, the occupant of the room with the bigger door will have a tendency to bully or dominate the resident of the other room.

~177~

MAINTAINING YIN AND YANG BALANCE IN ROOMS

Another dimension of feng shui is the need to maintain yin and yang balance. These are the two primordial forces that are opposite and yet complementary. Good feng shui can only exist when the two forces are correctly in balance.

To understand about yin and yang balance, it is important to realize that one gives existence to the other. Thus yin is darkness, night, cold, quiet, and stillness. Yang, on the other hand, is daylight, brightness, warmth, sounds, and activity. Thus, without cold, there is no warmth, and without sunshine, there can be no night time. Another attribute of the yin and yang cosmology is that one contains the seed of the other. Thus, in yang there must always be some yin and vice versa.

In feng shui, yin and yang balance requires the presence of both forces, but because we are dealing with life and energy when we speak of good feng shui, the environment should never be too yin. This creates lethargy and even death, yet it is necessary not to do away with yin altogether. Maintaining good balance between the two forces in feng shui requires great care and forethought.

The major directions of the home that affect children's luck are the east and the west. Make certain that the space that represents these two directions never gets too yin, for children's luck needs the energy, light, and life of yang.

This side of the home is completely overwhelmed. There is a high fence encroaching on the house, an overhanging roof which casts a shadow, and trees that have grown thick with foliage. Remove or lower the fence and thin out the trees to let in the sunlight!

A bright, cheerful room will attract positive energies and help your child to grow and develop.

Outside the home this happens when trees are allowed to grow out of hand, thereby completely blocking out the sunlight. When there is no sunshine, the environment becomes unhealthy. If the foliage of the trees creates excessive shade and darkness, the situation has definitely become too yin, to an extent that it may become harmful. Trim the trees and, if there are too many, thin them by cutting some down. This lets in the sunlight. Never allow trees outside the window of your children's rooms to block out the sun entirely. This causes sickness and, worse, lethargy, and depression.

Inside the home, space becomes too yin when rooms are damp and cold. This usually happens when store rooms or unoccupied rooms are not properly maintained. Never allow rooms to stay dark, cold, and damp for long periods. It is never good feng shui for the home and the first to be affected are usually the children of the household.

Children's rooms should have a good amount of yang energy. This is conducive to healthy growth and development. Paint the room in happy, bright colors. Install a music system or hang little chimes that make tinkling sounds.

Do not hang pictures or paintings of hostile faces or wild animals. The spirit of the predator is considered to be very real when symbols that depict it are present, so avoid such animals as tigers, leopards, and lions. The tiger is especially to be feared. Feng shui always warns against hanging pictures of them inside the home. They are excellent when hung outside the home, but there are very few people who can take the tiger into the house.

Keep pictures of tigers and other wild animals outside the home.

FEATURES THAT HURT CHILDREN

In their eagerness to practice feng shui, many people simply do not understand that they could well make tiny mistakes that have major consequences and these consequences often do not become immediately apparent. While it is generally known that water is good wealth feng shui, one great danger of activating it in the house, for example, is when it is placed under the staircase. This is a major taboo in feng shui. Never place any kind of water feature – a waterfall, fountain, or fish pond – under the staircase of the home. This destroys the luck of the second generation. Water under the staircase brings tragic consequences to the children of the household.

A water feature underneath the staircase hurts the children of the family. If you wish to decorate this area, place something solid here. This gives foundation to the home.

The position of toilets could affect the
future prospects of the children of the house.

TOILETS IN THE WRONG PLACES

If the toilet is in the southwest, it seriously blocks the marriage opportunities for the next generation. It will be difficult for the younger generation to find life partners. If the toilet is used by visitors, the effect is even more severe and girls in the family could well end up remaining spinsters. This feature also has very damaging effects on the marriage of the older generation.

A toilet in the west, which is of the metal element, causes general bad luck for your children. This is the corner that represents children's luck. Flushing the water away is especially harmful here because metal produces water – the metal element will become seriously exhausted.

The presence of a toilet in the east spoils the luck of the sons of the family, especially the eldest. In this corner, which is of the wood element, the effect of flushing away the water is even worse than in the west because water actually produces wood. It is like depriving the wood element of sustenance. The boys of the family get hurt and the health of the family will also suffer.

The best way of dealing with a toilet in the wrong place is to keep it closed. Better still, create some kind of divider that blocks off a view of the toilet. Small toilets are strongly recommended. In the old days, Chinese homes did not have toilets. This is because wherever they are located, they affect some kind of luck.

Feng Shui
Fundamentals

Education

THE MAJOR SYMBOLS OF EDUCATION SUCCESS

KEN

 The trigram that symbolizes knowledge and education is Ken, which essentially stands for late winter or early spring. It suggests a time of preparation upon which future success depends. Ken also suggests contemplation, meditation, and the development of the mind. When the energies within the home or room are harmonious within the corners that represent this trigram, excellent education luck can be activated.

THE DIRECTION NORTHEAST

Based on the Later Heaven Arrangement of trigrams around the Pa Kua, the compass direction that represents the trigram Ken is the northeast. Thus to activate education and study luck, it is necessary to energize the northeast.

The first thing to see is if there is a true northeast corner of the house. When houses are L- or U-shaped, certain corners appear to be missing and if this happens to be the northeast sector of the house, then feng shui suggests that the education luck of the home is generally lacking. While this can be unfortunate, there is no real cause for alarm.

Mark out the northeast corner using a compass. In this example, the northeast is marked out in yellow based on the compass reading shown. This will be the corner of the bedroom to activate.

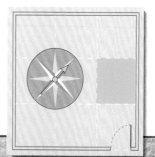

Go to the bedroom of the person whose education luck needs activating. This will usually be the bedroom of a child or young person who is still a student. Other rooms used by the entire family can also be activated. The first thing to do, if you wish your child to benefit from study luck, is to stand in the center of his or her bedroom and identify the northeast corner. Use the Lo Shu square as a guide for doing this. Divide the room into nine equal spaces. The bedroom does not need to be square. Two examples of doing this are shown here.

This is an irregular-shaped room, where the southwest is missing, and the south is partly missing. If the northeast corner had been missing, it would have meant an absence of education luck for the occupant of the room. The corner to be activated – the northeast – is drawn out in yellow. Note the method of demarcating the room into nine sectors.

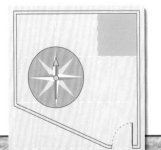

THE ELEMENT EARTH

The element of the northeast is earth. This is derived from the trigram Ken, which means mountain. Thus the element referred to is small earth, and to activate this corner, anything that symbolizes earth can be used. At the same time, we have seen from the cycles of the elements (see pages 24–5) that fire produces earth. This means that anything that symbolizes fire can also be used to energize the northeast. Earth produces metal and this means that metal exhausts earth. Metal would, therefore, not be a good energizer for this corner. It is inadvisable to place anything made of metal, including wind-chimes and bells, in the northeast corner. Finally, anything that belongs to the wood element should not be placed here, since wood destroys earth. This means that plants and flowers in the northeast will spoil your study luck.

~185~

ENERGIZING THE NORTHEAST WITH EARTH ELEMENT OBJECTS

The best way of energizing excellent study luck for the students in your family is to focus on energizing the northeast corner of their rooms with feng shui element therapy. Since the element of this corner is earth, displaying earth objects would effectively raise the chi to benefit their studies.

Place the work desk in the northeast of the room and place a crystal on it. This can be either a natural quartz crystal or a handmade lead crystal paperweight. Natural crystals are believed to have great retentive powers. Studying with the crystal nearby taps into the feng shui luck of the earth and the crystal itself will aid efficient study.

You can also work out the best personalized study orientation for your children (see pages 192–3). With this information, you will be able to arrange a child's or student's work desk to face in the ideal direction.

CRYSTALS

Place the desk in the northeast corner of the room and place a crystal on the northeast corner of the desk.

A natural quartz crystal is an ideal companion for every student who wishes to activate the earth element for good feng shui. These crystals come from deep within the earth's crust and are excellent purveyors of earth luck. Available from many museum or specialist shops, they are usually quite inexpensive.

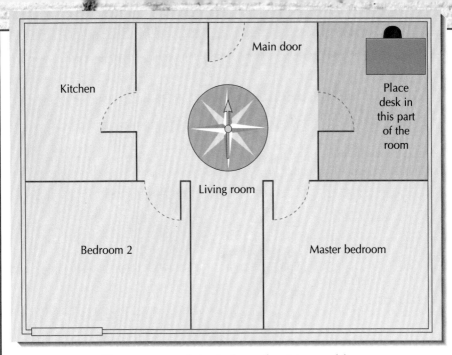

The corner room, being in the northeast, is one of the more suitable rooms for students since this corner symbolizes education and knowledge luck.

USING OTHER OBJECTS

Placing a decorative urn made of clay or any kind of pottery in the northeast is also excellent. It can be the northeast of the garden, the whole house, or the bedroom. Keep the urn empty so that good luck chi may accumulate and settle. Remember that this is the corner of small earth, so it is not necessary to place too large an urn.

Cut glass or crystal balls are also excellent activators when they are hung in the northeast, especially if there is a window and the facets catch the morning sunlight. This creates wonderful yang energy for the room and is especially auspicious.

LIGHTS AND LAMPS

A study lamp is excellent feng shui, but it is advisable to select it carefully. Try to avoid lamps that come in high-tech shapes that look threatening, for example, those with pointed ends or which are shaped in a hostile way. It is far better to choose a lamp that is rounded rather than angular. Do not use spotlights, as the yang energy then becomes too strong. A simple free-standing or hanging lamp is all that you require.

CRYSTAL CHANDELIERS

If you can afford it, perhaps the best way of energizing the northeast or any other earth corner of the home (the southwest and the center of the home) is to hang a beautiful crystal chandelier, as this combines the elements of earth and fire. Chandeliers with crystal pendants also attract sheng chi into the home when hung in the hall just in front of the main entrance door. If you cannot afford a crystal chandelier, shop for a cheaper substitute. Glass is as effective as crystal, as it is also of the earth element.

As an earth supplement, red furnishings and decorations are very effective, as the colour red symbolizes the fire element.

THE COLOR RED

This is an excellent way of supplementing earth with fire. Use red in drapes, cushions, or rugs, but never overdo it by painting entire walls in red since this will overwhelm the room. In feng shui less is better, as balance is essential. If the fire symbol is overdone, it will turn dangerous and burn you. In fact, this is true of every one of the five elements.

DESIGN MOTIFS

There are so many designs and motifs that can symbolize the fire element that you can be as creative as you wish. Designs that feature the sun or are created in red and yellow would be suitable. Again let balance prevail and if in doubt, have less rather than more.

STRENGTHENING THE EARTH ELEMENT WITH FIRE OBJECTS

Since fire produces earth in the cycle of element relationships, any kind of symbolic fire will strengthen the earth element, creating exactly the kind of auspicious flow of energy required. The element of fire is symbolized by all kinds of lights, sun motifs, and the color red. These are the common symbols that are also extremely easy to incorporate into the decor of any room.

ENERGIZING WITH OTHER SYMBOLS OF EDUCATION SUCCESS

Much of feng shui is very symbolic, which is why the Chinese have so many different emblems and gods that personify various aspects of human aspirations. There are gods of wealth and longevity, and symbols of fertility and purity, of undying love, and the attainment of affluence and power. And as you would expect, feng shui also has symbols of supreme educational success.

Practitioners of feng shui can choose to use the Chinese symbols or they may use, equally successfully, symbols that strongly suggest educational success to them. Hence hanging pictures and crests of universities along the education wall (the northeast wall) can be very effective. So, too, is displaying any diplomas, qualifications or awards which reveal your parents' achievements. This attracts knowledge chi into a household that demonstrates what a profound respect it has for education. In this way, the parents' success will be guaranteed to continue to the next generation.

THE WHITE ELEPHANT

This is one of the great treasures of Buddhism and in Thailand the elephant is regarded as a sacred animal. It is a symbol of strength, prudence, and sagacity. Displayed in the home, the feng shui significance borders on the almost superstitious belief that it aids the sons of a family in gaining recognition through determination and prudence. This belief is widespread in Vietnam and Cambodia, where ceramic white elephants are a popular feature of most homes. Place them in pairs just outside the doorway.

The white elephant personifies the virtues of strength, prudence. and sagacity. This powerful symbol is found in many homes in the East.

~190~

THE DRAGON CARP

The Chinese regard this as the most potent symbol of education and career success. The symbol is that of a creature with the tail of a carp and the head of a dragon, which symbolizes the humble carp transforming into a dragon. Dragon carps, which can be ceramic or made of wood, are usually displayed in pairs placed on either side above the entrance into the home. This symbolizes that each time the residents go out of the home to face the world they become brave and clever dragons! The dragon carp crossing the Dragon Gate is thus also very popular for activating career luck.

THE FOUR PRECIOUS TREASURES

Also referred to as the invaluable gems of the literary apartment, the four treasures are ink, paper, brush pen, and ink slab. When present in the home, these items signified the presence of a learned man. Thus, in the old mansions of Chinese mandarins, they were always specially displayed with great care, and in most instances, were of the finest quality. Chinese ink was usually stored in solid form, hence the ink slab. Paper was often made from the finest rice straw, while the brush pen was made of sable, fox, or rabbit hairs set in a bamboo holder. If you display these four items in your home, it is believed that at least one of your children will gain the highest scholastic achievements.

Ink, paper, brush pen, and ink slab are displayed in the home to assure educational success.

PERSONALIZED STUDY ORIENTATIONS

THE COMPASS FORMULA

According to feng shui, each person has four lucky and four unlucky directions, depending on whether he or she is an east or west group person. Which group you belong to is determined by your year of birth and gender. Once you know the personal auspicious Fu Wei direction of your child, you can make use of the information in many different ways that will greatly enhance his or her personal feng shui luck.

It can be used with equal success in the various rooms of the home, the classroom, in school, and at college. Using the direction implies sleeping and sitting in a direction that allows the person to capture his or her Fu Wei. Doing this successfully leads to great success in any endeavor, which requires the enhancement of the intellect and the development of a skill or profession. It brings recognition, achievement, and success to those who genuinely work at securing this success. The Fu Wei direction imparts precious feng shui luck which consider-

ably smoothes the way to success. Your child will feel energized and highly motivated and will catch the eye of teachers.

This formula is thus ideal for those who want to become grade A students and who have ambitions to climb to the very top of their profession. It is not for

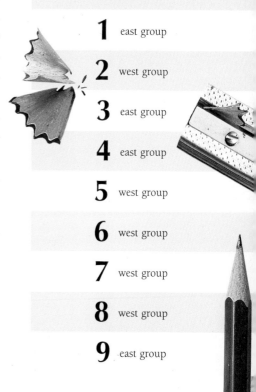

If your Kua number is:

1 east group

2 west group

3 east group

4 east group

5 west group

6 west group

7 west group

8 west group

9 east group

enhancing incomes as much as for personal growth and development, although implicit in this sort of luck is the promise of great success in the future.

YIN AND YANG
FOR GROWING CHILDREN

To enjoy good feng shui, rooms and houses should have a mix or balance of both yin and yang. An excess of yin suggests stillness, stagnation, and even death, while an excess of yang suggests hyperactivity.

Your Fu Wei orientation is:

NORTH for both males and females

SOUTHWEST for both males and females

EAST for both males and females

SOUTHEAST for both males and females

SOUTHWEST for males and **NORTHEAST** for females

NORTHWEST for both males and females

WEST for both males and females

NORTHEAST for both males and females

SOUTH for both males and females

THE KUA FORMULA

To determine your orientation, first determine your Kua number

▨ Obtain your Chinese year of birth based on the calendar on pages 30–1 and use this calculation to get your Kua number.

▨ Add the last two digits of your Chinese year of birth. e.g. **1948, 4+8=12**.

▨ If the sum is higher than ten, reduce to a single digit, thus **1+2=3**.

Males: Subtract from **10**, thus **10-3=7**.
So, for men born in **1948**,
the Kua number is **7**.

Females: Add **5**, thus **3+5=8**.
So, for women born in **1948**,
the Kua number is **8**.

Now check against this table for your Fu Wei direction and location.

There is no 5 in this formula, though it is shown in the table for clarity. Females should use 2 instead of 5, and males 8.

Growing children need yang energy, but they also need yin energy when they sleep. Thus their rooms should essentially be bright, airy, and filled with life. This can be achieved using sounds (a music system), and a bright color scheme (drapes, rugs, quilts), or paintings and pictures that show life, but of course this should not be done to excess.

ACTIVATING THE FU WEI DIRECTION

Once you know your child's personal Fu Wei direction and you have demarcated your floor area according to the Lo Shu square, there are several ways you can start to match his or her human chi energies with that of the surrounding space. The Fu Wei direction can be activated to attract auspicious sheng chi for personal benefit.

Check the Fu Wei direction based on his or her Kua number from the table on page 193. This is also the luckiest compass location for your child's bedroom. Tapping the Fu Wei allows your child to sleep, eat, and study well, without succumbing to the stresses and strains of work or exams. Incorporating this formula into his or her personal feng shui is also a very effective safeguard against carelessness, ill health, and laziness.

The ideal way of capturing good study luck with this method is to try to match all the most important doors in the home according to your child's Fu Wei, but this is hardly practical. Nor is it very clever; other members of the family must also be taken care of and account must be taken of the overall luck of the family. Leave the main door into the home for other feng shui features that benefit every member of the family, especially the breadwinner or head of the household.

Concentrate, instead, on using your child's personal Fu Wei direction for his

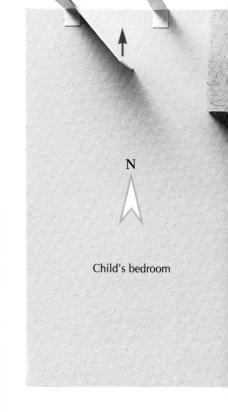

N

Child's bedroom

or her room. The direction your child faces when sleeping, sitting, and working should follow his or her personal auspicious direction. This means working with the following:

Desk

Bed

The arrows indicate how the sleeping and working directions should be oriented. Note that for sleeping, where the head points is vital, and for sitting down to work, where the head faces is important. In this example, even the door into the bedroom points to the Fu Wei direction; this is excellent, but it is not always possible to get everything right. Two out of three is fine!

THE FU WEI DIRECTION IN PRACTICE

For example, if your child's Fu Wei direction is north, this is how he or she should sleep and work.

▨ The door into his or her bedroom.
▨ The placement of his or her bed to tap the best sleeping direction.
▨ The placement of the desk to tap the best working direction.

IN THE GARDEN

Extend element theory into the garden. Install a high light in the northeast corner of the garden to activate education luck for your children. Repeat this garden light also in the south, which represents the luck of recognition. This attracts success luck in examinations and should be of assistance when your children apply for

such things as scholarships and study grants. Do this early in your child's school career and let the effect be felt gradually over the following years.

ACTIVATING FU WEI
IN SCHOOL AND IN COLLEGE

The auspicious direction can be applied all through life. Carry a small compass everywhere you go and develop the habit of always taking directions. This makes it easy to identify your best education direction each time you sit down to take an exam. If possible, choose a desk in the classroom that is auspicious for you.

At university, simply move the position of the desk and bed in your room to tap into this powerful method of feng shui. Even if you do nothing else except guard against feng shui's killing breath, your hard work will be handsomely rewarded with excellent academic success.

A simple pocket compass, like those used by Boy Scouts, is an enormously valuable aid for enhancing your education luck.

FENG SHUI DURING EXAMINATIONS AND INTERVIEWS

The auspicious direction method can, and indeed should, be activated in other situations. Whenever possible, let your child face this direction

- When doing his or her homework or when revising.
- When sitting for an examination.
- When attending lectures or in class.
- When attending interviews.

LOOKING OUT THE WINDOW

If the study desk is positioned so that the child looks out of the window and is directly facing an oncoming road, a dead tree, or the edge of a large building, the view can be the source of severe shar chi. Use heavy drapes to block it out.

THINGS TO BE ALERT TO

It is important to remember that the luck of the good direction by itself does not represent any protection against shar chi caused by beams, pillars, and sharp edges. These are structural features present in any building and it is important to develop a habit of always noticing where they are, so that you can avoid them.

In addition, you should also be alert to the less obvious structures, features, and objects that may be sending out secret poison arrows. For instance, if there are paintings of guns hanging on the walls, these send out negative energy. Paintings,

EXAMS

Examination success depends above all on thorough and conscientious preparation. But sitting in an auspicious direction, protected from the harmful effects of any poison arrows that may be in the room, will ensure the best results possible.

Trees too close to the window, thereby blocking off the sunlight, create excessive yin energy which can be harmful. They need to be chopped down or at least cut back. However, if trees are not too close and look healthy and the direction outside is the east, they can be a most auspicious view. Just make certain trees never block out the sun completely. If the trees are in your garden, trim them each year to maintain good balance and harmony.

especially abstracts, that seem negative or hostile can be disastrous. For example, Picasso's Weeping Woman is a particularly bad painting to hang anywhere near children. The defensive dimension of feng shui should never be ignored. Even if everything else is correct, the killing breath of symbolic poison arrows is extremely harmful and it can, in certain circumstances, be lethal.

Carry a compass everywhere and when attending lectures, try to sit facing your study direction, that is, your Fu Wei direction. If this is not possible, at least make certain that you do not sit facing one of your four unlucky directions, as this will simply drain you of energy, thereby affecting your powers of concentration. Let the energies around work for you, rather than against you.

During exam times, be extra careful with your sitting direction. Check the

Wall paintings of guns, or other hostile objects, can have a very negative effect in a classroom, study, or examination room.

orientation of the room and, if possible, swivel your chair so that you take your examination facing at least one of your four auspicious directions. This will ensure that your sitting direction is in harmony with the energies that surround you during that crucial testing time.

HAZARDS AND HOW TO SPOT THEM

THE CHANGING ENVIRONMENT

Much of feng shui practice is getting accustomed to spotting structural features inside and outside the home which can harm members of the family. It is often easy to overlook this defensive aspect. Hazards in the immediate external environment require the main entrance door into the home to be protected. Inside the home, hazards are created by structural pillars, beams, the layout of the rooms, and the arrangement of furniture. It is, therefore, necessary to familiarize yourself with at least some of the more common dangers that may inadvertently threaten to destroy all the good feng shui so painstakingly put in. In fact, it is advisable to be aware of changes in the environment in and around the home so that the family's feng shui is never at serious risk.

New roads can create potentially hazardous poison arrows. It is important to be attuned to these types of changes in our surroundings because they may affect home and family.

Feng shui is not a static exercise. Because the energies within the environment are constantly changing, living in a state of awareness is important. For example, when trees are small they blend in beautifully with the surroundings, but as they grow, the energies emitted are expanded, eventually causing imbalance not only of yin and yang, but also in the five element cosmology. In the same way, new roads, new buildings, and infrastructure developments will always have a strong feng shui significance.

There are two aspects to being alert to the changing forces in the environment. The first concerns being aware of physical changes and the second has to do with intangible forces caused by nothing more than the passage of time. Both aspects are dealt with in this book.

THE BRIGHT HALL

Feng shui often speaks of the benefits that accrue from having an empty space in front of the home. Such an empty space – a park, football field, or playground – allows the beneficial and benign sheng chi to accumulate and settle before entering your home, bringing good fortune with it. The phrase used to describe this feature is the bright hall. When there is a bright hall in front of your main door, your family will enjoy great good fortune and all plans will proceed smoothly.

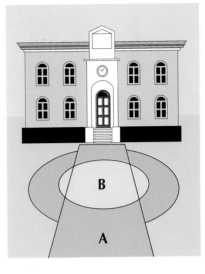

Schools and colleges with a playing field or empty land located directly in front of the main entrance usually produce excellent graduates. This good fortune is caused by the bright hall effect, which brings excellent feng shui to the school. However, if there is a straight road leading directly toward the main gate **A**, the effect is extremely inauspicious. It is far better to have a circular driveway, as this slows down the energy coming toward the building **B**. Good chi always moves slowly. Bad chi always moves fast.

PHYSICAL CHANGES IN THE LANDSCAPE

A new highway overpass will definitely hurt your family if it seems to cut into your home. For rooms that face such an overpass, the harmful hostile energies will be too strong, causing severe bad luck. The construction of a new high-rise building also affects the feng shui of a home. If the new building blocks the main door, the effect will be negative. If it rises behind your home, thereby symbolizing solid support, then the effect is good feng shui. Generally, as most infrastructure projects are massive, they cause severe bad luck when they are located in front of your home.

THE CHINESE VIEW OF EDUCATION

Chinese history is filled with stories about scholars. In ancient China, the path to high office and probably the only way for young men from humble backgrounds to positions of power was to pass the Imperial exams. Attaining a high level of scholarship was metaphorically likened to the lowly carp successfully crossing the Dragon Gate and transforming into a dazzling dragon.

The legend of the dragon carp accurately encapsulates the Chinese attitude toward education, which is one of deep respect. Right up to today, the most important thing to Chinese families throughout the world is that their children should excel in their studies. Like their ancestors of old, they see the scholastic route as the most efficient way of improving their status and their lifestyle. It is hardly surprising that immigrant Chinese in the United States, Britain, and all over Southeast Asia place the attainment of tertiary qualifications by their children as the number one priority in their young lives. A high-quality education has always been considered the universal key to success.

Getting a tertiary education is regarded as the necessary first step in their path to prosperity. Success in exams is viewed as more than a mere end in itself. It is the vital first step in carving out a substantial life and career.

THE ROLE OF FENG SHUI.

It is hardly surprising that one of the most important dimensions of feng shui practice focuses not just on the next generation (the descendants), but more specifically on their attainment of knowledge, which manifests itself in conspicious success at examinations. In the modern context this can be interpreted as getting

good grades all the way through school and into university.

Indeed, there are specific feng shui recommendations that directly address this matter of crossing the Dragon Gate. Both form school and compass feng shui offer exciting methods and guidelines, which are easy to implement, to benefit your children's scholastic career.

THE NATURE OF STUDY LUCK

Today's educational process is as demanding as that of the old days of Imperial China and given the huge competition for university places, excellent examination grades have become immensely important. In the face of all the things that can go wrong, a little help from good feng shui cannot be anything other than welcome. Activating study luck can help remove some of the examinaton hurdles that every student faces, but it is not magic. Remember that it does not automatically turn your child into a straight A student, but with good feng shui, efforts pay off and hard work will show real results. Feng shui is the luck from the earth. If your child complements it with the luck created by his or her own efforts, quantum leaps in achievement will definitely be experienced.

The humble carp, successfully crossing the Dragon Gate and transforming into the magnificent dragon, symbolizes the humble scholar passing the Imperial exams, thereby setting forth on the path to power and high position.

Feng Shui
Fundamentals

Networking

SYMBOLS THAT ACTIVATE POWERFUL PATRONS

THE DIRECTION NORTHWEST

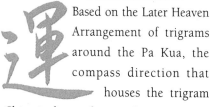

Based on the Later Heaven Arrangement of trigrams around the Pa Kua, the compass direction that houses the trigram Chien is the northwest. Thus to activate the luck that brings influential friends, mentors, and advisers into your life, it is necessary to energize the northwest.

The first thing to investigate is whether there is a northwest corner of your home

When homes are L- or U-shaped, certain corners are missing. If the missing corner happens to be the northwest sector of the house, then feng shui suggests that the all important Chien luck missing.

If you wish to benefit from Chien luck, stand in the center of the home and from there identify the northwest corner. Use the Lo Shu square as a guide for doing this. Divide the home into nine equal spaces. It does not need to be square – two examples are shown here.

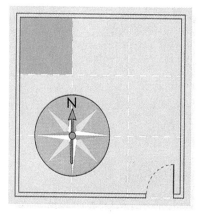

Mark out the northwest corner using a compass. This will be the corner of the home to activate. A main door placed here would not be bad at all, but a toilet located here would be disastrous.

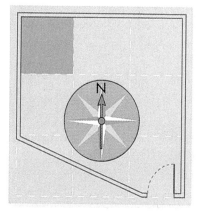

This is an irregular-shaped house. The southwest is missing and the south is partly missing. A missing northwest corner would mean an absence of mentor-luck for the members of the family. The corner to be activated – the northwest – is indicated.

CHIEN

The trigram of power cannot be anything but Chien, the one that symbolizes heaven. It signifies the ultimate yang energy and stands for intrinsic and spiritual strength. It represents the leader, king, commander, and patriarch, the man of power who possesses a divine right to rule. Chien is a very powerful trigram. It epitomizes the spirit of the creative, and the energy of neverending movement and relentless activity. It is described in the I Ching as the root of all other trigrams because all three lines are unbroken, solid, and yang. Chien personifies a person of great power, who is also wise and compassionate.

In feng shui, activating this trigram has many benefits, chief among them is the luck of having someone wise to advise you and someone powerful to help you. During your auspicious astrological period, it could even bring an influential mentor into your life who will support and promote you.

The placement of Chien on the Pa Kua – its direction and location – indicates the important elements to energize. In doing so, it is important to know that Chien becomes even more auspicious when combined with the trigram Kun, the ultimate yin trigram. The pairing of the ultimate yang with the ultimate yin is irresistibly auspicious. The element of Kun is big earth, which produces big metal, the element of Chien.

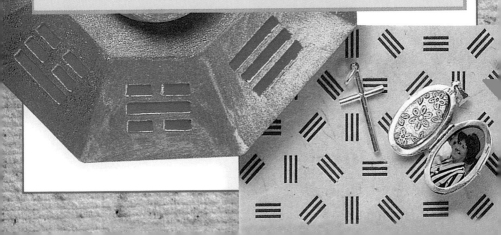

WINDCHIMES

Large windchimes, made of steel or copper that give off attractive tinkling sounds, are highly effective when activating the northwest because the music they make creates sheng chi. It is important that the rods are hollow because this allows the chi to rise and circulate through the home, bringing good fortune.

There are different types of windchimes. Those sold in Chinese emporiums are usually made of copper or bronze and they are fashioned as pagodas and good-luck carp designs. Western-manufactured windchimes are usually better made and create beautiful chords and melodies that reverberate through the home. Use either type to activate the northwest. Hang them high up near ceilings so that they catch the wind more easily. Ceramic windchimes are also effective, but do not use wooden windchimes (because wood is destroyed by metal).

ACTIVATING THE METAL ELEMENT

The element of Chien and, therefore, of the northwest is big metal. Anything that typifies metal can be used to activate this corner.

At the same time, because earth produces metal, anything that connotes earth, especially big earth (the trigram Kun), is also appropriate. Remember, that fire destroys metal, and is therefore construed as being harmful to Chien. So anything that signifies the fire element should not be placed here.

ELECTRIC FANS

Ceiling fans made of metal are excellent energizers for the northwest. Apart from being made of metal, the movement of the blades creates wind and activity, which also symbolize vital yang energy. Free-standing fans are also effective and antique fans are especially good!

Place metal objects in the home to activate the northwest corner.

OTHER METAL OBJECTS

Place metal objects in the northwest in the living and family rooms. Equipment, such as stereos and televisions, have feng shui value when they are placed in this corner. Decorative bells and horseshoe magnets are also good supplementary display objects that enhance the corner effectively.

Never place lamps, candles, spotlights, or anything that suggests the fire element in the northwest corner. This signifies fire at heaven's gate (see pages 38–39) and can cause great problems. Always remember that fire destroys metal and the larger the fire object, the more harmful it is. Not only is networking-luck destroyed and occluded, but this will cause grave imbalance within the family household. Those people involved in professions for whom support from the top is vital should be especially careful about this particular feng shui taboo.

Any object displayed for feng shui purposes should be tied with red thread. This attaches yang energy to the object, symbolically making it come alive. It is then more effective and meaningful.

STRENGTHENING THE METAL ELEMENT WITH EARTH

Since earth produces metal in the cycle of element relationships, symbolic earth will strengthen the metal, creating exactly the kind of auspicious energies required. The element of earth, especially big earth, also connotes the trigram Kun, the ultimate yin trigram. When Kun is brought together with Chien, the pairing represents the unity of heaven and earth – a most auspicious combination.

Placing decorative ceramics in the northwest is an excellent method of stimulating the earth element because they are made of sand and clay. The object can be an urn, a figurine, or any of the good-fortune symbols. Most ceramic objects originating from China or Hong Kong have colorful illustrations on them.

The exact placement should be the northwest corner of a room, the entire home, or the garden. In the case of an urn placed in the garden, keep it empty so that good luck chi may accumulate and settle. The examples illustrated are a few suggestions that can be decorative and have excellent feng shui value at the same time.

CRYSTAL FISH

There are large collections of glass or crystal fish that come in beautiful colors. Since the fish itself is an excellent good-fortune symbol, placing a medium-sized specimen on a northwest table is excellent. Large numbers of metal (brass) carp are made by the cottage industries of Thailand and Burma. Placing a pair in the home or incorporating them in water features, such as fountains and ponds, is an excellent landscaping idea and has great feng shui potential.

LUCKY CERAMIC FROG

Usually made of clay and colored gold, the lucky frog is generally depicted as the legendary three-legged frog sitting on a bed of gold coins. Place this symbol in the northwest to attract excellent wealth- and career-luck, as well as mentor-luck. Frogs, in general, represent good fortune.

DECORATIVE BELL

Often decorated with elaborate motifs and carvings, bells made of clay or metal are used very effectively to activate the northwest of a room. Place a bell on a table top or in a display cabinet. Bells represent the announcement of glad tidings and good fortune.

DECORATIVE URN

Urns are usually made either in brilliant, solid colors or illustrated with peonies, storks, and legendary figures. An urn is excellent placed in the northwest or near the entrance of the home to welcome in the good-fortune sheng chi. It can be as large as you wish, but it is wise to keep the concept of balance in mind. Never allow decorative objects to overwhelm the home.

STATUE OF BUDDHA

These statues are extremely popular with antique collectors. One made of clay can be placed in the northwest to stimulate luck from heaven. Statues of deities (of whatever religion or culture) should always be placed on a platform or table. They should never be placed on the floor, as this would be most disrespectful. Newly-made statues are preferable to antique ones, since old Buddhas, especially Buddha heads, may have a spiritual history that carry harmful negative energies.

The Chinese tradition of displaying portraits of ancestors to bring protective luck can be imitated by Western families.

ENERGIZING WITH OTHER SYMBOLS OF MENTORS

Much of feng shui is very symbolic. This is why the Chinese have so many different emblems and gods that personify aspects of human aspiration. There are gods of wealth and longevity and symbols of fertility, purity, undying love, and the attainment of affluence and power. There are also symbols of supreme educational achievement.

Practitioners of feng shui can choose to use the Chinese symbols or they may, with equal success, use symbols that strongly suggest powerful and successful leaders of their own traditions. Hanging pictures of traditional heroes on the northwest wall can be very effective. Many Chinese homes also display specially commissioned portraits of ancestors. These are usually placed prominently in the reception rooms to great effect for tuning into protective luck.

OTHER CULTURAL EQUIVALENTS

Choose from your own cultural and historical background. All the great traditions of the world have their own folk-heroes and legendary figures. Thus British homes can display paintings or statues of great military heroes or any of the monarchs from their rich history whom they admire or who are an inspiration to them. The French can display Napoleon, the Americans can choose from among their past presidents. These statues represent people whose achievements or position can signify the kind of luck desired. They can be made of metal or clay, but avoid placing statues carved out of wood in the northwest corner.

KUAN KUNG

The Chinese are also fond of displaying statues of the famous legendary heroes from the days of the three kingdoms, such as Kuan Kung, who was deified many years ago as the God of Wealth and Protection. Kuan Kung statues stand proudly in many Chinese homes and offices, as his countenance is believed to impart protection and support from powerful people.

Religious homes can display a painting or sculpture of their religious or spiritual leader. Hang it in the northwest because such a picture can represent divine blessings from heaven. Remember that feng shui is not spiritual. It is best treated as an ancient practice that aims to create and harness positive, auspicious energies within the living space. Any object or painting, which creates these energies, will attract good fortune.

The three solid lines that represent the trigram, Chien, can also be displayed to great effect in its own northwest corner. The medium can be embroidery or paint or the trigram can be incorporated into ceiling designs.

The trigram can be painted or embroidered or it can be incorporated into ceiling designs.

ACTIVATING SYMBOLIC SUPPORT

Arranging the feng shui of the home to attract powerful friends and mentors into our immediate circle must always incorporate a simple yet profound feng shui tenet: "mountain behind and water in front."

The mountain behind creates symbolic support for the home, ensuring from the start that the natural forces of the environment are protecting, rather than confronting you. This is the central dogma of form school feng shui, which describes the back support as the black turtle hills. These hills (preferably located to the north) should have a gentle gradient and be rounded in shape to represent the back of the longevity turtle. In cities, a large building behind your home can symbolize this important mountain support. If the building is in front of your home – facing your main door – not only will your luck be blocked, but you will be severely lacking in support. You cannot enjoy real networking-luck of any kind, no matter what other precautions you take.

THE GREEN DRAGON HILLS OF THE EAST

There should also ideally be a range of dragon hills on your left (preferably the east side of your home). These hills should curve gently round your home, as if they are holding it in a protective embrace. The hills should be gently undulating, slightly lower than the turtle hills, but higher than the hills on the right-hand side.

THE WHITE TIGER HILLS OF THE WEST

The hills on the west should have a gentle slope and curve round the home as well. However, they must never be higher than the other hills around you, otherwise the spirit of the tiger overwhelms that of the dragon and the turtle, thereby turning on the home itself and bringing very bad feng shui indeed.

In front of the home, there should be a view of water and a small elevation of land to represent the presence of the legendary crimson phoenix, the celestial creature that always brings immense good fortune. Beyond the phoenix footstool should be a view of gently flowing water – a brook, river, lake, or canal. If the water flows from left to right, the feng shui created for the home will be so auspicious it is said that the good luck will last for at least five generations.

Form school feng shui maintains that the armchair or horseshoe composition created by these three ranges of hills represents the classical formation necessary for excellent feng shui. Residents will enjoy wealth, rank, power, and influence. Patronage from the top comes with little effort, and from apparent coincidences, bringing endless opportunity for advancement.

The ideal setting for a home has mountains behind, water in front, and gentle hills to the west and east.

INDIVIDUAL SUCCESS ORIENTATIONS

PATRONAGE

To the Chinese, enjoying the patronage of powerful mentors is a highly regarded asset. Much of Chinese fortune-telling focuses on whether one's destiny offers this kind of luck.

The Chinese believe that patronage or networking-luck comes from heaven. To illustrate this, they point to the emperors, in particular of old China, who were said to rule with a mandate from heaven. The rise and fall of imperial dynasties reflected this divine decree being given or withdrawn.

THE FOCUS OF FENG SHUI

Feng shui recognizes the importance of having the support and encouragement of mentors and helpful people in order to enjoy great and longlasting success. Consequently, it offers specific guidelines for energizing our living space to produce this very special luck.

The methods focus on creating the presence of powerful mentors whose help pulls the family upward to high positions

If your Kua number is:

1	east group
2	west group
3	east group
4	east group
5	west group
6	west group
7	west group
8	west group
9	east group

of wealth and influence. Patronage-luck in ancient China can be likened to networking-luck in the commercial world of today. Success still depends a great deal on the support we attract from managers, leaders, and anyone in authority.

Luck is always an intangible factor and networking-luck is particularly valuable. Good feng shui will give you a significant edge over everyone else!

Your Success orientation is:

SOUTHEAST for both males and females

NORTHEAST for both males and females

SOUTH for both males and females

NORTH for both males and females

NORTHEAST for females and **SOUTHEAST** for males

WEST for both males and females

NORTHWEST for both males and females

SOUTHWEST for both males and females

EAST for both males and females

THE KUA FORMULA

Calculate your Kua number as follows. Add the last two digits of your Chinese year of birth. e.g. **1978**, **7+8=15**. If the sum is higher than ten, reduce to a single digit, thus **1+5=6**.

Males	**Females**
Subtract from	Add
10	**5**
thus	thus
10-6	**5+6**
=4	**=11**
So, for men born in	then
1978	**1+1**
the Kua number is	So, for women born in
4	**1978**
	the Kua number is
	2

Now check against the table for your success direction.

GOOD FENG SHUI AT WORK

It is not a good idea to have exposed book shelves around. They represent knives cutting into you. Placed behind, they are even more deadly. Put doors on your book shelves or arrange your books so that they blend with the shelves.

Having the door behind you is extremely bad feng shui. It means that even people you trust will betray you. It is very harmful to career luck.

Be careful what you put on your desktop. Avoid items that are pointed and have their edges pointing at you. Flowers are excellent and so, too, are crystals and other good-fortune symbols. Place them according to the compass sectors of the desk itself. Thus, place the table lamp on the south part of the desk and any flowers on the east side.

Wear colors that make you strong and energetic. Find out the ruling element of your Chinese year of birth from the calendar on pages 30–1, then plan your wardrobe to include colors that are good for you. Red is good for those who need fire, such as people born in a wood year at the height of winter. Winter wood needs the warmth of fire. Wear black and blue for water, green for wood, yellow and beige for earth, and white for metal.

DESK DIMENSIONS

There are auspicious and inauspicious dimensions in feng shui. Lucky desk dimensions can actually help you gain promotion. These dimensions are based on the feng shui ruler. Experience shows that the desk most conducive to excellent career luck is one that is 33 x 60 x 33 inches (84 x 152 x 84 cm). The dimensions suggested are excellent for working people, but there is some room for variation.

Desk lengths can vary according to your job. The following sets of dimensions have been chosen to ensure you will make absolutely no errors. Vary between 57 and 61 inches (145 and 155 cm), between 41 and 44 inches (104 and 112 cm), and between 49 and 52 inches (124 and 132 cm).

Those who find the height suggested uncomfortable can place a platform under the chair or under the desk itself. Feng shui dimensions can also be applied to cabinets, cupboards, doors, and windows. Carpenters in Hong Kong, Singapore, and Malaysia all use the feng shui ruler, which has to date been available only in Chinese, to make certain the furniture they make conforms to the correct feng shui specifications.

There are also inauspicious dimensions, which create problems associated with stress, illness, and tension. Some of these dimensions can also cause loss and betrayal. It is worth adjusting your office furniture to avoid these problems.

If the dimensions of your desk conform to feng shui specifications, your career luck will be enhanced.

CHECKING COMPATIBILITY

EAST AND WEST GROUP PEOPLE

相容

The Kua formula used in compass feng shui offers one of the most accurate ways of investigating the degree of compatibility between people. It is particularly useful for investigating romantic relationships, but can also be used for checking the degree of your compatibility with your colleagues, friends, and supervisors.

The simple rule is that people of the same group, east or west, tend to collaborate well. If your mentor belongs to the same group as you, the relationship requires less effort on your part because the natural energies are compatible. When an east group person has a west group mentor (or vice versa), he or she should work harder at the relationship.

Depending on the Kua numbers of both, however, incompatibility can sometimes be so severe as to make the

COMPATIBLE KUA NUMBERS

Your Kua No.	Sheng Chi Kua	Tien Yi Kua	Nien Yen Kua	Fu Wei Kua
1	3	4	1	9
2	7	8 (m) 8&5 (f)	2&5 (m) 2 (f)	6
3	1	9	3	4
4	9	1	4	3
5	7 (m) 6 (f)	8 (m) 2 (f)	5	6 (m) 7 (f)
6	8 (m) 8&5 (f)	7	6	2&5 (m) 2 (f)
7	2&5 (m) 2 (f)	6	7	8 (m) 8&5 (f)
8	6	2&5 (m) 2 (f)	8 (m) 8&5 (f)	7
9	4	3	9	1

Successful working relationships will be guaranteed if the compatibility of people's groups is taken into account.

relationship too difficult to get anywhere. The tables on pages 220 and 222 reveal the degrees of compatibility and incompatibility between people of different Kua numbers. Use them to check the compatibility between you and the people who are important to you. Remember that the gender of the person you are investigating is relevant to the formula.

Males with Kua number five should follow the numbers with (m) after and females with Kua number five should use the numbers with (f) after. This grid refers to Kua numbers that are compatible with your Kua number. You will see that east group people respond well to others of the east group and west group people with others of the west. The degree of compatibility is described as follows:

※ **Sheng Chi Kua:** extremely compatible. This person brings you excellent luck. He or she makes a powerful and trustworthy friend, manager or mentor.

※ **Tien Yi Kua:** this person looks after you well and the relationship is non-stressful. You can confide in him or her and there is always trust between you.

※ **Nien Yen Kua:** a harmonious relationship. This person can be relied on to look after your interests.

※ **Fu Wei Kua:** this person is good for you. He or she is supportive, encouraging and especially good at developing your talent to its fullest potential.

WARNINGS OF INCOMPATIBILITY

Note: males with Kua number 5 should follow the numbers with (m) after and females should follow the numbers with (f) after. The numbers in the grid refer to Kua numbers that are incompatible with your Kua number. Again, note that east group people are incompatible with west group people and vice versa. These numbers refer only to Kua numbers and nothing else.

The degree of incompatibility is described as follows.

▨ **Ho Hai Kua:** this person is not very good for you. He or she will cause you to have accidents and mishaps. The relationship is not smooth and there are constant misunderstandings, but problems are not insurmountable. If your mentor belongs to this Kua in relation to your Kua, overlook petty issues that cause friction and try to work at the relationship.

▨ **Wu Kwei Kua:** very incompatible. You will have plenty of disagreements. There is anger and hidden resentment in the relationship. This is the five ghosts association, suggesting that outside parties will succeed in causing problems between you. Be careful.

▨ **Lui Sha Kua:** extremely incompatible. This person will cause you grievous harm and immense problems. This is the six killings description and could be dangerous. Be very careful.

INCOMPATIBLE KUA NUMBERS

Your Kua No.	Ho Hai Kua	Wu Kwei Kua	Lui Sha Kua	Chueh Ming Kua
1	6	2&5 (m)	7	8&5 (f)
2	9	1	3	4
3	8&5 (m)	7	2&5 (m)	6
4	7	8&5 (f)	6	2&5 (m)
5	9 (m) 3 (f)	1 (m) 4 (f)	3 (m) 9 (f)	4 (m) 1 (f)
6	1	9	4	3
7	4	3	1	9
8	3	4	9	1
9	2&5 (m)	6	8&5 (f)	7

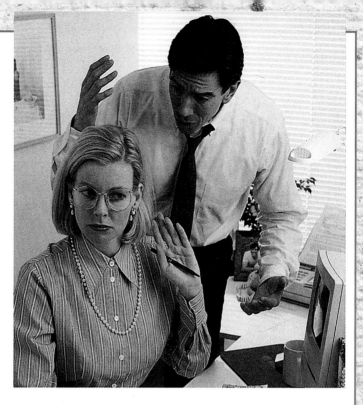

Incompatible Kua numbers could result in tension and conflict between work colleagues.

▓ **Chueh Ming Kua:** This person could be the death of you, figuratively and metaphorically. He or she could ruin your name and cause you loss of income and position. Stay well clear of this one, no matter how promising the friendship or relationship seems to be at the start. Over the long term, this person will have no qualms about betraying you totally. Remember this does not mean that he or she is a bad person per se; it is simply that your Kua numbers are totally and irretrievably incompatible.

The east and west group formula to determine compatibility between people complements the astrological method, which uses the Chinese ghanzhi system of heavenly stems and earthly branches (see pages 224–5). This system is more popularly recognized by the Chinese zodiac animal signs. On rare occasions, although the Kua formula and the ghanzhi system indicate compatibility, sometimes the elements (wood, fire, water, metal, and earth) of the birth charts can completely override the readings, causing problems between seemingly compatible people. Similarly, the elements of the birth chart can override seeming incompatibility, but again these are rare occurrences.

CHINESE ASTROLOGY COMPATIBILITY

In Chinese astrology, every person is said to belong to one of 12 zodiac animals, which represent one year in a cycle of 12 years. The animal sign you belong to depends on your year of birth. These are referred to as the earthly branches. The 12-year cycles are repeated five times to represent the five elements, fire, wood, water, earth, and metal. These elements are designated as heavenly stems. Together, this makes up a cycle of 60 years: 12x5=60. This is termed the ghanzhi system.

Every lunar year is therefore described in terms of branches and stems – animals and elements. The year 1997, for example, is the year of the ox and the element is earth. Thus, everyone born in the lunar year 1997 is said to be an earth ox.

CHECKING THE HEAVENLY STEMS

The productive cycle of the five elements (page 25) indicates compatibility. The destructive cycle of the five elements (page 25) indicates incompatibility.

CHECKING THE EARTHLY BRANCHES

Animals that belong to each of the four triangles of affinity are compatible.

- The competitors of the horoscope are the rat, the monkey, and the dragon. Their ambitions are totally compatible.
- The independent spirits are the horse, the dog, and the tiger. They understand each other perfectly.
- The intellectuals are the snake, the rooster, and the ox. They always have time for each other.
- The diplomats are the rabbit, the sheep, and the pig. They are kindred spirits.

All animals that are directly opposite each other are said to be incompatible. This means a six-year age gap is incompatible:

- Rat and Horse
- Ox and Sheep
- Tiger and Monkey
- Rabbit and Rooster
- Dragon and Dog
- Snake and Pig

These animal signs will always find it hard to work together harmoniously. There are hidden resentments.

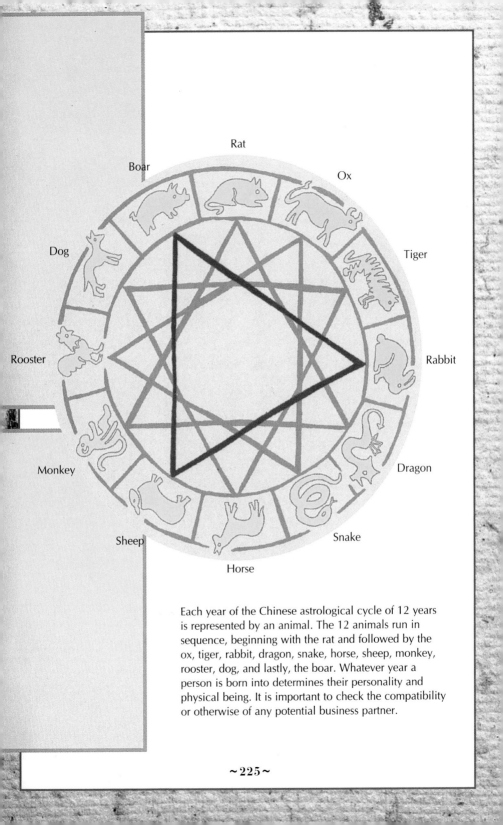

Each year of the Chinese astrological cycle of 12 years is represented by an animal. The 12 animals run in sequence, beginning with the rat and followed by the ox, tiger, rabbit, dragon, snake, horse, sheep, monkey, rooster, dog, and lastly, the boar. Whatever year a person is born into determines their personality and physical being. It is important to check the compatibility or otherwise of any potential business partner.

Feng Shui
Fundamentals

Careers

FENG SHUI FOR CAREERS

THE DIRECTION NORTH

The trigram that represents careers is Kan and, according to the Later Heaven Arrangement of trigrams, this is placed in the north. This is therefore the corner of any home or room that represents career prospects and career luck. If this corner has good feng shui, residents will have the good fortune to attain great heights in their careers.

Understanding the nature of career luck requires an examination of the north sector of the room or home and, in particular, the meaning of the trigram Kan.

THE WATER ELEMENT

The ruling element of the north is water, symbolized by anything liquid and also by water features, such as aquariums, pools, lakes, and fountains.

▧ Water is produced by metal, so metal is said to be good for it.

▧ Water itself produces wood, so wood is said to exhaust it.

▧ Water is destroyed by earth, so earth is said to be harmful to it.

▧ Water destroys fire, so it is said to overcome fire.

From these attributes, we know that to strengthen the element of the north, we can use all objects that symbolize both water and metal. Also, we should strenuously avoid anything belonging to the earth element. This means that the north may be activated by any object, color, or painting that suggests water or metal.

This is probably the most dangerous of all eight trigrams. It is made up of one unbroken, yang line embraced by two broken, yin lines. This is a trigram that looks weak and yielding outside but, in fact, can be very strong inside.

Kan symbolizes the cold of winter, the danger or opportunity of water, and the cunning of the middle son. It can represent either illusions – like the moon's reflection in water – or great success through a person's ability to hide his or her strength and appear weak – the essence of cunning that is the sum and substance of this trigram.

This trigram represents situations of entanglement and a perpetual position of danger. Kan perfectly encapsulates the scenarios in ancient China when court intrigues often resulted in great danger for the mandarins who vied for promotion. One false step and death was the result; hence this trigram represents career luck.

To enjoy a smooth and successful climb up the career ladder it is vital to activate this corner of your home and room, as well as your office. By guarding the feng shui of your north corner you will be protecting yourself from getting hurt by intrigues, deceit, and trickery. Good feng shui will ensure that sincerity of purpose is rewarded – so that the yang line sandwiched between the yin lines will stay strong and not be overcome.

THE MAJOR SYMBOLS
OF CAREER SUCCESS

ENERGIZING THE WATER ELEMENT
IN THE NORTH

In feng shui, each of the five elements is activated when objects that belong to the element group are present. To energize the water element of the north career corner, one of the best and easiest methods is to use small, artificial water features.

You can include water in a room in many different ways. If it is very small, an aquarium or fountain might create imbalance; in this case, all you need is a vase filled with water and flowers or a bowl of water. Any decorative item that has colored or moving water can be used to stimulate the water element. The important factor to bear in mind is never to overdo things or go overboard. If you create a large artificial water feature in your living room, for instance, it might look very spectacular, but it will overwhelm all the other energies. Instead of activating the element, the water will drown you, causing you to suffer all the negative consequences of poor feng shui.

However, you should note that while the water corner can be activated effectively to enhance careers, this should be confined to your living room or office. Fountains and aquariums should never be placed in the bedroom. Feng shui tradition states that an aquarium that is placed behind your bed may cause you to be robbed or cheated.

If you can afford it, install a small water fountain against the north side of your living room wall. There are many different designs available and all that is needed is a small pump to create a continuous flow of water.

An aquarium makes an excellent water energizer. Fish swimming about and an oxygenator creating bubbles ensure the water is moving. Stagnant water creates stagnant chi and this is worse than not having water at all. Place a light above the aquarium, as this creates the movement of shadows on the ceiling.

WATER MOTIFS AND COLORS

These can be incorporated into the overall interior design of your living room. Make them look esthetically pleasing. The colors of the north sector are black or any shade of blue to reflect the water element. Incorporate this color scheme into wallpaper, drapes, and rugs. The north wall itself can also be painted in any shade of blue. Lighting in this corner should be subdued.

As a rule, feng shui Masters usually advise against having a swimming pool in the home. This is not because it is inauspicious, but simply because if you place it in the wrong sector of your plot, its shape is wrong, or its size creates massive imbalance, it is likely to do a great deal of harm to residents. It is very easy to get swimming pools wrong.

A swimming pool in the grounds of a large house, however, can bring extremely beneficial energies if everything is done right. It must be placed correctly, fashioned in an auspicious shape, and its size should balance both the house or building and the grounds.

Locate a swimming pool in the north, east, or southeast of your grounds. It can be extremely harmful and cause

If this pool is in the north corner of your land, the location is acceptable and can be auspicious. However, if from inside the house looking out, it is on the right-hand side of the main door, this could cause strife in the relationship of residents. Also the pool is too large for the size of the house and is too near it. Swimming pools have to be very carefully planned.

Kidney-shaped or circular pools are auspicious. Best of all, is to allow the pool to embrace the home.

problems if it is located in the south. It is also more auspicious when it is in a position where it can be seen from the main door. For women, the advice is that a swimming pool should never be on the right of the main door (seen from the inside looking out). If it is on the right, a husband will develop a roving eye and become unfaithful.

Round and circular shapes are considered superior to rectangular pools with pointed corners. The best shape is kidney-shaped or like a double eight; one whereby the pool seems to be embracing the house. When a house is embraced by water, especially water that appears to come from the north, it is an excellent feng shui feature.

If you have a swimming pool on your land, ensure that it is visible from at least one of the doors of the home. It is also vital that the water is kept clean. There is nothing more damaging to the feng shui of a home than a body of dirty and polluted water. This allows the precious chi to become stale and harmful, causing the home's residents to suffer from ill health and loss. There can be no career luck when this happens.

ENERGIZING THE TURTLE

A small pond with a live turtle or terrapin is better than a swimming pool. In fact, if you want to make certain you will never be lacking in support in your job, you should symbolically invite the celestial turtle into your home. If a terrapin pond in the north side of your garden is impractical or if you live in an apartment, buy a ceramic turtle and place it in a bowl of water in the north corner of your home or living room. This is one of the easiest and most effective methods of energizing excellent career feng shui. You will never lack support and it will create a great deal of goodwill and respect for you at the office. The turtle is also a symbol of longevity and having him in the home energizes health as well. Keep only one turtle (or terrapin) since the lucky number of the north is one.

The turtle is a symbol of career support, as well as longevity.

SYMBOLS OF THE METAL ELEMENT

The Chinese word for metal also means gold. In feng shui, gold does not just represent money. It is also the symbol of prominence and affluence. Symbols that stimulate this element when placed in the career corner are believed to bring great success to those engaged in public life.

INSIGNIA OF RANK

In the old days of imperial China, court mandarins wore robes embroidered with insignia to signify their rank. Nowadays, wealthy Chinese collect well-preserved antique robes that have their insignia intact to hang in their homes. They are thought to produce an auspicious aura in which the cosmic currents can generate favorable good luck that leads to elevation in rank. Other decorations and success symbols can be used for the same purpose.

COINS

Coins can be really effective for activating the north corner. For this purpose it would be excellent to use old Chinese coins with a square hole in the center, but it would be easier to use the ordinary coins you find in your small change. Set aside a small, decorative box, preferably one that is made of metal – brass, pewter, or silver – and keep all your leftover change inside. Place this box anywhere in the north corner. A variation on this idea is to use an antique metal bowl containing leftover coins.

Coins will stimulate the metal element and encourage career luck if they are placed in the north corner.

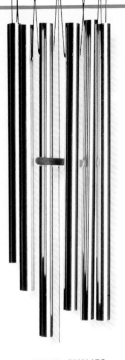

MAGNET

Horseshoe-shaped magnets are universal good-fortune symbols. Place one on the floor, under or inside a cupboard. This symbolizes gold hidden within and is believed to symbolize good luck.

BELL

Bells are very symbolic of high position. If you are hankering after a promotion, get a small silver- or gold-colored bell and hang it on a wall in the south or you can place a dinner bell on the south side of the dining room to activate the good luck of that corner each time you sit down for supper.

WIND CHIMES

These have several uses in feng shui since they are believed to be effective cures to dissolve the negative influence of beams and sharp-edged corners. Hung in the north, they are also excellent for attracting auspicious chi that creates good fortune for those who wish to advance in their careers.

Windchimes placed in the north should be made of metal and the rods should be hollow. This allows the chi to be channeled to the corner. Windchimes with solid rods have no feng shui significance. The number of rods in the windchime should ideally be one of the good luck numbers – one, six, seven, or eight. It is not advisable to hang windchimes that have five rods.

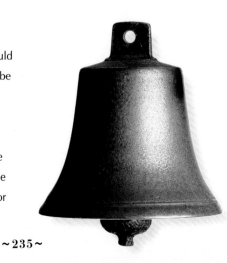

INDIVIDUAL CUARER ORIENTATIONS
INDIVIDUAL
CAREER ORIENTATIONS

YOUR SELF-DEVELOPMENT
CAREER DIRECTION

方
位

The auspicious career direction of every person is known as the fu wei direction. Once you know your personal fu wei direction, you can make use of that information in many different ways to enhance your personal feng shui. You can use it with equal success in your home, as well as in the office. Essentially this means sleeping and sitting in a direction that allows you to capture your fu wei. Capturing the luck of your direction implies embarking on a career path that leads to phenomenal success within your chosen profession. You will feel capable and energized at work and really start to enjoy being there. You will catch the eye of your manager and promotion will seem a foregone conclusion.

This formula is most suitable for people who are interested in pursuing a career and who have ambitions to climb to the very top. It is not for enhancing income as much as for personal growth and development, but implicit in good

career luck is a significant improvement in your standard of living.

CAREER SUCCESS –
A CHINESE PERSPECTIVE

There is a Chinese legend that tells of the humble carp that swims against the current up the Yellow river until it reaches the Dragon Gate, or lung men, and

If your Kua number is:	
1	east group
2	west group
3	east group
4	east group
5	west group
6	west group
7	west group
8	west group
9	east group

then, in one mighty leap, it strives to make it to the other side, crossing the Dragon Gate. Those who made the leap were transformed into dragons, while those who did not would forever bear the sign of failure, a large red dot on the forehead.

From the legend arose the belief that a dragon gate should be built to symbolize career success. These gates were usually adorned with carps that had the heads of dragons and the bodies of fish to signify their transformation to a more elevated status. It is still possible to find them in old mansions that belonged to the most prominent mandarins in ancient China.

THE KUA FORMULA

Calculate your Kua number as follows. Add the last two digits of your Chinese year of birth. e.g. **1948**, **4+8=12**
If the sum is higher than ten, reduce to a single digit, thus **1+2=3**

Males	Females
Subtract from	Add
10	**5**
thus	thus
10-3	**5+3**
=7	**=8**
So, for men born in	So, for women born in
1948	**1948**
the Kua number is	the Kua number is
7	**8**

Now check against this table for your career direction and location.

Your Career orientation is:

NORTH for both males and females

SOUTHWEST for both males and females

EAST for both males and females

SOUTHEAST for both males and females

SOUTHWEST for males and
NORTHEAST for females

NORTHWEST for both males and females

WEST for both males and females

NORTHEAST for both males and females

SOUTH for both males and females

Career luck in feng shui must be seen from the perspective that it does not refer to wealth, although a higher standard of living is implicit in career success. Career luck means attaining greater rank, power, authority, and ultimate influence.

CORPORATE FENG SHUI

THE CORPORATE HEAD OFFICE

Corporate feng shui always begins with protective measures to deflect or dissolve the effects of any killing chi caused by pointed or hostile structures aimed at the entrance of the head office. Protect the entrance doors, block off these hidden poison arrows, and, where necessary, retaliate with a strategically positioned Pa Kua mirror or even a cannon.

The cannon is a very powerful defensive tool in feng shui and should not be used lightly, since it causes extremely bad feng shui for any residence or office hit by it. However, when the offending structure is the edge of a massive building or other sharp arrow-like structure, you may have no choice but to use a cannon. If you do, make sure it is pointed directly only at the offending structure. Place it outside your building as a decorative object. Use an old cannon but if you cannot get your hands on a genuine one, a model will do just as well.

Use either a real cannon or a model of one to deflect the effects of killing chi.

TIPS FOR FINANCIAL SUCCESS

A Try to have a small plot of empty land, such as a playground or park, directly in front of the building. This empty space is termed the auspicious bright hall, where good-fortune chi can settle and accumulate before entering the building. If this is not possible, then at least make sure the entrance does not feel cramped or overwhelmed by the buildings surrounding it.

B Try to avoid being squeezed between two taller buildings. If you are, place a very bright light on the roof of your building and switch it on every day at nighttime.

C If a straight road approaches your building, re-orient the door so that the straight and pernicious energies of the road – like tigers in the night – cannot enter your building. If you can, place a wall of water, flowing inward toward the building, between the road and your entrance.

D If a new building is erected in front of your building, causing your company's fortunes to flounder, take remedial action immediately. Either re-orient your own building completely by changing the entrance direction or use the cannon. Alternatively, you can install plenty of lights and big fountains to attract chi toward your building, despite any blockages that it may experience.

E If there is a river flowing near your building, make every attempt to orient your front door to face it and get the compass direction to match with the flow of the water. If the river flows past the back rather than front door, you will miss every opportunity to grow, expand, and flourish.

F If there are escalators directly facing the entrance to your building, ensure that they move in a well-lit and landscaped atrium. Escalators leading to an open space force fast-moving, inauspicious energy to become gentle and auspicious. Otherwise, they can cause problems for the company.

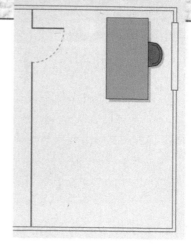

FENG SHUI IN THE OFFICE

Even if your offices are overcrowded, success will come by following some simple feng shui ground rules.

- Reception areas should be well lit. The receptionist should sit with her back to a wall blocking the general office from view of the entrance.
- Do not arrange desks in a confrontational manner – one directly facing the other. It is better if office colleagues sit side-by-side.
- Arrange the desks in such a way that there is a meandering flow in the traffic.
- Avoid having too many partitions that result in long corridors being created in the layout. This leads to quarrels, backbiting, and disharmony in the office.
- Do not station key personnel in rooms that are located at the end of a long corridor. If the finance director sits there, your company's finances will be affected. If the marketing director sits there, sales will be adversely affected.

BAD DESK PLACEMENT:

- The desk is too near the door
- The occupant sits with his or her back to the door
- The occupant is sitting with his or her back to a window.

GOOD DESK PLACEMENT:

- The desk is diagonal to the door
- The occupant is facing the door
- A solid wall is behind the occupant.

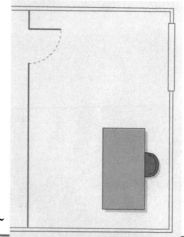

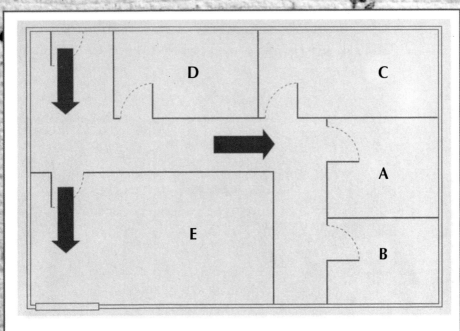

Follow feng shui rules to maximize success in the office environment.

The receptionist should sit with her back to the wall.

OFFICE PLACEMENT

A Is an inauspicious office location.

B Is the best as it is diagonal to the entrance.

C Is a good location for the boardroom.

D Is too near the door.

E Shows two doors in a row with a window in the general office. This could not be worse.

GOOD RECEPTION AREA.

Chi is forced to meander upon entering the office. The receptionist is sitting with the solid support provided by the wall.

THE CHIEF EXECUTIVE'S OFFICE

- ▨ Destroy any poison arrows by eliminating protruding corners, free-standing pillars, open book shelves, and overhead beams.
- ▨ Activate the wealth corner of the office with a healthy and vibrant plant in the southeast.
- ▨ Arrange the office so that the chief executive can sit facing his or her wealth direction (check the Kua number). What is good for the chief executive is good for the company.
- ▨ Keep the office well lit. Place a light in the south corner to ensure success in all executive decisions.
- ▨ Place a painting of a mountain behind the chief executive to ensure that he or she has support at all times.

THE BOARDROOM

The feng shui of the boardroom is important for a company's fortunes simply because major decisions are taken there. The success of the company can be adversely affected if there is killing breath present in this room, either caused by protruding corners or because windows open to offensive structures that allow shar chi to enter.

Check the chairperson's seating placement. This should preferably be away from the entrance, with his or her back properly supported by a solid wall.

Do not have too many doors opening into the boardroom, as this leads to quarrels and misunderstandings, and is not conducive to the generation of wealth.

Let each member of the board sit in his or her wealth direction. This enhances the feng shui of the company.

FENG SHUI
FOR MANAGERS

NEGOTIATING DIRECTIONS

Use the Kua formula directions to load the dice in your favor in every aspect of your work. Always carry a small compass and try to sit facing your best career direction when you are negotiating an important contract. It may not get you everything you want, but it will seriously increase your chances of getting a good deal. You can also use the same method when making a speech, negotiating your year-end bonus, or simply interviewing for a job.

negotiation
on the telephone

AUSPICIOUS TRAVEL DIRECTIONS

When planning your business trips – in fact, every time you travel in connection with work – try to plan your route and your calls to come from your auspicious direction. This applies to world travel by plane or local travel by car. Coming from your good direction means you are bringing luck with you!

With international travel, the direction you fly from depends entirely on the route you take. Thus, flying from the United States to Asia, you can travel eastward or westward. Check your directions carefully if the trip is an important one. This method should definitely be used if you are relocating for a few years.

sales meetings management meetings training sessions

Each time you find yourself on a podium addressing an audience – at a sales convention, at a budget meeting, in a training session – try to orient your body so that you are facing your best career direction. This allows you to receive the auspicious energies in the room. Your audience will be very receptive and positive. The session will be a success.

At job interviews and office meetings, make it a habit to face your career direction when you speak. If this is not possible, at least face one of your four good directions.

interviews divisional meetings

Always sit facing your best direction when you negotiate. Make it a habit until it becomes second nature. Be extra careful that you are not facing any of your inauspicious directions

IMPROVING THE BOTTOM LINE

Those who work in sales or marketing or have profit responsibility – sales people, branch officers, or insurance agents – can use feng shui to improve turnover and profits. This can be done through feng shui methods that address prosperity luck.

ENERGIZING THE UNIVERSAL WEALTH SECTOR

The universal prosperity corner is the southeast of any room, office, or retail establishment and energizing this sector of the room attracts good fortune chi for the business or company. Place a plant in the southeast corner of your office or store. Make it a beautiful healthy plant, not one that looks half dead – and make sure it stays healthy. If it starts to get sickly, remove the yellowing or dead leaves and, if necessary, replace it altogether. Fake plants made of silk will be equally effective, but do not allow dried plants or flowers in the southeast whatever happens.

Plants and water features enhance good career luck when placed in the prosperity corner of the company or business.

Place a healthy plant in the
southeast corner of the
office or store
to energize
prosperity.

ACTIVATING
THE ORDER BOOK

An extremely useful feng shui tip that
managers of retail branch establishments
can use is to activate the order or sales
book. This involves the use of three old
Chinese coins. These coins have a small,
square hole in the center. The square and
the circular shapes together represent the
harmonious unity of heaven and earth.
Place the three coins, yang side up (the
side with four characters is yang, while
the side with two characters is yin), then
tie the three coins together in any shape
you like with thick red thread. The red
thread is important as this energizes the
flow of chi. Stick the coins on top of your
order book. This method increases
turnover and is an especially useful tip
for sales people.

The three coins with red thread method
can be used just as effectively with
important files. Customer files, for example,
can be activated in this way. These coins
can also be hung above the main door on
the inside. Get these coins (they are very
inexpensive) from your local
Chinese supermarket.

A small water
feature, such as a
fountain, will also
activate career luck.

GLOSSARY

C

Chen The Arousing trigram, whose direction is east and number is 3.

Chen Lung Pak Fu Green dragon/white tiger formation.

Chi The life force or vital energy of the universe. Chi can be either auspicious or inauspicious.

Chien The Creative trigram, whose direction is northwest and number is 6.

Chueh Ming Literally, "total loss of descendants," the location that represents the worst possible kind of disaster or bad luck that can befall any family.

Compass School The Feng Shui school that uses compass formulas to diagnose the quality of Feng Shui directions and locations.

Confucius The renowned Chinese philosopher (551–479 B.C.) and great moral teacher, who spent a lifetime studying the *I Ching*.

D

Dragon's cosmic breath
see **Sheng Chi**

E

Early Heaven arrangement One of the two Pa Kua arrangements, used when considering the Feng Shui of Yin dwellings, or the abodes of the dead.

Eight Life Aspirations method A method of allocating corners in a room that identifies various life aspirations.

Elements The five elements in Chinese belief – earth, wood, fire, metal, and water – that provide vital clues to the practice of Feng Shui.

F

Feng Shui Literally, "wind/water," the Chinese system of balancing the energy patterns of the physical environment.

Flying Star Feng Shui The formula that determines good and bad time dimension Feng Shui for homes and buildings based on the Lo Shu square.

Form School The Feng Shui school that focuses predominantly on the contours of physical landscapes – their shapes, sizes, and courses.

Fu Wei Literally, "overall harmony," the location for achieving peace.

Fuk The Chinese god of wealth and happiness.

H

Hexagram A figure of six lines, of which there are 64 in the *I Ching*, symbolizing the universal archetypes of human consciousness.

Ho Hai Literally "accidents and mishaps," the location that leads to financial loss and intermittent difficulty.

I

I Ching A Chinese classic known in the West as *The Book of Changes*.

K

Kan The Abysmal trigram, whose direction is north and number is 1.

Ken The Mountain trigram, whose direction is northeast and number is 8.

Killing breath *see* **Shar Chi**

Kua One of the eight sides of the Pa Kua. Each individual's Kua number identifies auspicious and inauspicious locations.

Kun The Receptive trigram, whose direction is southwest and number is 2.

L

Later Heaven arrangement One of the two Pa Kua arrangements, used when considering the Feng Shui of Yang dwellings, or abodes of the living.

Li The Clinging trigram, whose direction is south and number is 9.

Lo Shu The magic square, comprising an arrangement of nine numbers into a three-by-three grid, which first appeared about 4,000 years ago on the back of a turtle. The square exerted a powerful and mythical influence on Chinese cultural symbolism.

Lui Sha Literally, "six killings," the location that represents grievous harm to you and your family.

Luo Pan The Chinese Feng Shui compass, which contains all the clues and symbols that indicate good or bad Feng Shui. Luk The Chinese god of high rank and affluence.

N

Nien Yen Literally, "longevity with rich descendants," the best location for enhancing the quality of home life and family relationships.

P

Pa Kua The eight-sided symbol used to help interpret good or bad Feng Shui. It corresponds to the four cardinal points of the compass and the four sub-directions and derives its significance from the eight trigrams of the I Ching.

Pa-Kua Lo-Shu theory The theory, based on the Pa-Kua and Lo-Shu, that every abode can be divided into eight sectors, each representing an auspicious or inauspicious situation.

Poison arrow Any sharp or straight structure from which foul energy or Shar Chi emanates, carrying with it ill fortune and other odious effects.

S

Sau The Chinese god of health and longevity.

Shar Chi Literally, "disruptive Chi from the west" or inauspicious energy lines, caused by the presence of sharp, pointed objects or structures that channel bad Feng Shui; also known as "killing breath."

Sheng Chi Literally, "growing chi from the east" or auspicious energy lines, which travel in a meandering fashion. Also known as "dragon's cosmic breath" or benign breath.

Sheng Chi When referring to a location, literally "generating breath," the best location for attracting prosperity.

Sun The Gentle trigram, whose direction is southwest and number is 4.

T

Tao "The Way," a philosophy and way of life – the eternal principle of heaven and earth in harmony.

Tao Te Ching An important Chinese philosophical text, traditionally ascribed to Lao Tzu, and one of the keys to philosophical Taoism.

Taoism The philosophical system set forth in the *Tao Te Ching*.

Tian ling di li ren he The six-character phrase meaning "auspicious heavenly influence, beneficial topography, harmonious human actions" that is often used to describe Feng Shui in classical texts.

Tien Ti Ren Heaven luck, earth luck and, man luck.

Tien Yi Literally, "doctor from heaven," the best location for members of the household who are ill.

Trigram A figure made up of three lines, either broken or complete, which symbolizes the trinity of heaven, earth, and man.

Tui The Joyous trigram, whose direction is west and number is 7.

W

Water Dragon Classic A formula that offers twelve water flow and exit directions across a plot of land; also the title of one of the source texts for Feng Shui practice, about the relative merits of waterways.

Wu Kwei Literally, "five ghosts," the location that generates the kind of bad luck that results in fires, burglary, and loss of income or employment.

Y

Yang Creative energy, one aspect of the complementary opposites in Chinese philosophy. It reflects the more active, moving, warmer aspects; *see also* **Yin.**

Yang Dwelling Classic One of the classic Feng Shui manuscripts, which lays down guidelines on house and room positioning.

Yang Yun-Sang, Master Principal advisor to the court of the Tang emperor Hi Tsang (A.D. 888) and widely acknowledged as the founder of Feng Shui.

Yin Receptive energy, one aspect of the complementary opposites in Chinese philosophy. It reflects the more passive, still, reflective aspects; *see also* **Yang.**

FURTHER READING

Kwok, Man-Ho and O'Brien, Joanne, *The Elements of Feng Shui,* ELEMENT BOOKS, SHAFTESBURY, 1991

Lo, Raymond *Feng Shui: The Pillars of Destiny (Understanding Your Fate and Fortune),* TIMES EDITIONS, SINGAPORE, 1995

Skinner, Stephen, *Living Earth Manual of Feng Shui: Chinese Geomancy,* PENGUIN, 1989

Too, Lillian, *Basic Feng Shui,* KONSEP BOOKS, KUALA LUMPUR, 1997

Too, Lillian, *Chinese Astrology for Romance & Relationships,* KONSEP BOOKS, KUALA LUMPUR, 1996

Too, Lillian *Chinese Numerology in Feng Shui,* KONSEP BOOKS, KUALA LUMPUR, 1994

Too, Lillian, *The Complete Illustrated Guide to Feng Shui,* ELEMENT BOOKS, SHAFTESBURY, 1996

Too, Lillian, *Dragon Magic,* KONSEP BOOKS, KUALA LUMPUR, 1996

Too, Lillian *Feng Shui,* KONSEP BOOKS, KUALA LUMPUR, 1993

Too, Lillian *Practical Applications for Feng Shui,* KONSEP BOOKS, KUALA LUMPUR, 1994

Too, Lillian *Water Feng Shui for Wealth,* KONSEP BOOKS, KUALA LUMPUR, 1995

Walters, Derek *Feng Shui Handbook: A Practical Guide to Chinese Geomancy and Environmental Harmony,* AQUARIAN PRESS, 1991

USEFUL ADDRESSES

Feng Shui Design Studio
PO Box 705, Glebe, Sydney, NSW 2037, Australia, Tel: 61 2 315 8258

Feng Shui Society of Australia
PO Box 1565, Rozelle, Sydney
NSW 2039, Australia

The Geomancer
The Feng Shui Store
PO Box 250, Woking, Surrey GU21 1YJ
Tel: 44 1483 839898
Fax: 44 1483 488998

Feng Shui Association
31 Woburn Place, Brighton BN1 9GA,
Tel/Fax: 44 1273 693844

Feng Shui Network International
PO Box 2133, London W1A 1RL,
Tel: 44 171 935 8935,
Fax: 44 171 935 9295

The School of Feng Shui
34 Banbury Road, Ettington,
Stratford-upon-Avon, Warwickshire
CV37 7SU. Tel/Fax: 44 1789 740116

The Feng Shui Institute of America
PO Box 488, Wabasso, FL 32970,
Tel: 1 407 589 9900 Fax: 1 407 589 1611

Feng Shui Warehouse
PO Box 3005, San Diego, CA 92163,
Tel: 1 800 399 1599 Fax: 1 800 997 9831

INDEX